Occult Mead

The Author Transgressing via
the Guise of a Notorious Occultist

Occult Mead

Essays on Runes, Grails, and the Round Table Sun Wheel

Eirik Westcoat

Skaldic Eagle Press
Long Branch, Pennsylvania
2025

Copyright © 2025 Eirik Westcoat
All rights reserved.

For permissions or other information, please contact the author at <eirik@theskaldiceagle.com> or <www.theskaldiceagle.com>.

The cover icon is a rendering of the sun wheel design found in Wewelsburg Castle. See the acknowledgments on page vi for details and copyright. All layout and design by Eirik Westcoat.

First Edition, Winter Nights 2025

9 8 7 6 5 4 3 2

Color Trade Paperback
ISBN: 978-1-947407-17-6

Skaldic Eagle Press
Long Branch, Pennsylvania

*For the Once-and-Future
Guild of the Grail*

Acknowledgments

Thanks go to several persons unnamed for their reading and comments on this book prior to publication. Thanks go also to my Patreon subscribers who saw drafts of five of these essays in advance.

Certain characters in foreign and ancient language words which are not in the main typeface used for this book have been changed to more common alternate versions. These include the use of ö instead of the medieval form with the small descending hook.

The Wewelsburg sun wheel image used as the cover icon and at the end of the text is my remixed version (altering only the colors and adding a core to the center of the design) of the one by the user Blacksonne on this page:
<commons.wikimedia.org/wiki/File:The_Black_Sun.svg>.
It is copyright 2016 and available via a Creative Commons license, CC BY-SA 4.0, <creativecommons.org/licenses/by-sa/4.0/>. My remixed version is released under the same license and available in digital format at <www.theskaldiceagle.com>. I call this symbol the Round Table Sun Wheel. Other image credits are with their essays.

Several of the essays here have inspired poems published in the companion book to this one, *Shining Mead: Poems Inspired by Life, Conjunction, and Occultism*. These are the essays on Moldavite, Eagle and Gar, Triadic Experiences, and the Wewelsburg symbol. I encourage my readers here to check out that volume as well.

Lastly, this book would not be possible without the three guiding stars of my Work: Óðrœrir, Rûna, and the Grail.

Table of Contents

Preface xii

Odian Wandering Among the "Ettins": Support for Exploring Wherever the Adventure Leads

Opening Remarks 1
Odian Wandering in the Lore 1
Applying Odian Wandering 3
Is Odian Wandering Welcome Today? 4
Transmuting My Christian Heritage 7
Evola and the Guild of the Grail 9
What about the Whataboutism? Countering the Sophists ..11
Another Example: The Millerman School 15
A Short Recap 18
Final Remarks 19
Works Cited 20

Moldavite as the Stone and the Grail

Introduction 23
Why Gemstones? 23
Moldavite: Exoteric Properties 24
The Grail Stone According to Wolfram and Others 27
The Alchemical Stone According to VandenBroeck 29
The Stone Revealed? 31
Alchemical Implications 32
Moldavite: General Esoteric Properties 33
General Possibilities for Esoteric Work 35
Speculative Old Norse Possibilities for Esoteric Work 36
Conclusion 37
Works Cited 37

Eagle and Gar: Enhancing One's Rune-Work with These Powerful Symbols
Introduction 39
The Eagle 40
The Gar 46
Conclusion 50
Works Cited 51

The Canon of Nine: A Spiritual Call to Arms
Introduction 53
How to Approach the Precepts 53
1. "Adherence to antiquity is superior to acceptance of modernity" 56
2. "Self-overcoming is superior to self-acceptance" ...58
3. "Seeking the unattainable is superior to surrendering to the commonplace" 59
4. "Struggle and strife are superior to comfort and passivity" 61
5. "Imitation of the great is superior to paltry innovation" 63
6. "Right action is superior to personal convenience" 65
7. "To be strong and alone is superior to being weak and consorted" 66
8. "The aristocratic is superior to the egalitarian" 68
9. "Nobility and restraint are superior to plebeianism and vulgarity" 70
Wrap Up: A Call to Arms 71
Works Cited 72

Towards a Meta-Order of Tradition: The Once-and-Future Guild of the Grail
Introduction and Rationale 73
Definitions and Concepts 73
Orders and Traditions 75
The Meta-Order of Tradition 78
To What Further End? 82

Conclusion 83
Works Cited..83

The Quartets of the Elder Futhark and Anglo-Saxon Futhorc: A Sixfold of Creation, Society, Nature, Cosmos, Divinity, and World

Introduction 85
Clarifications of Time and Futharks 86
First Quartet: Creation..87
Second Quartet: Society..89
Third Quartet: Nature...91
Fourth Quartet: Cosmos 93
Fifth Quartet: Divinity..95
Sixth Quartet: World 97
Conclusion 98
Works Cited..99

The Fourth Ætt of the Anglo-Saxon Futhorc: Triads of Initiation, Knighthood, and Mastery

Introduction 101
The Runes of the Fourth Ætt 102
The First Triad: Preparedness and Virtues 103
The Second Triad: Transitions 104
The Third Triad: Grail Hallows 106
Conclusion: The Path of Initiation 108
Works Cited..109

Triadic Experiences for my Triple Quests: Examining Revelatory Singularities on My Esoteric Path

Introduction 111
The Concept of the Rûna-Experience............................111
Back Story: A Persistent Interest in Poetry and Óðrœrir 113
My Own Rûna-Experience: The Reality of Óðrœrir 115
My Wode-Experience: An Encounter with the Mead Force....116

Did I Hear a Word?..118
My Grail-Experience: Another Irruption of Power 119
Analyzing the Triad 121
Thirty-Three, New Runes, and an Initiatory Catalyst 124
Conclusion 127
Works Cited...128

Wewelsburg's So-Called "Black Sun" is Really Himmler's Round Table and Grail

Introducing the Infamous Wewelsburg Sun Wheel................129
An Impossible Nut to Crack? 131
Describing the Wewelsburg Symbol 132
The Wewelsburg North Tower..136
The Wewelsburg Castle Itself..141
The Unrealized Future Plans for the Site 146
Heinrich Himmler: The Boss Man Himself...........................148
Karl Maria Wiligut, Occultist on Staff 152
Wiligut's Naming Rite and the Death's Head Ring................154
The Historical Silence Regarding the Symbol's Meaning 156
Wiligut's Santur: Could a Black Sun Actually Be Involved? 157
Archaeological Antecedent: The Zierscheibe...........................158
The Vision of the Grail at the Round Table 161
The Winchester Roundtable..163
The Round Table in the Wigalois of Wirnt von Grafenberg....164
Wigalois and the Wheel of Fortune 165
Art Imitates Unknown Prior Art 168
The Grail: The Color Green from Wolfram 170
Wiligut's Reversed Sun-Runes 170
The Perfect Storm in 1938 172
Putting It All Together: The Mystery Solved.........................175
A Restatement: The Three Layers of the Symbol's Meaning....179
Some Notable Implications of All This..................................180
Critiquing Faulty Depictions 181
Re-Naming the Symbol..182

Depicting the Symbol Going Forward 183
Liberating the Round Table Sun Wheel: Why Now & Me? 185
Final Remarks 188
Acknowledgments 189
Works Cited 189

Preface

"One has to take a somewhat bold and dangerous line with this existence: especially as, whatever happens, we are bound to lose it."
—Friedrich Nietzsche

"Myth is not prehistory; it is timeless reality, which repeats itself in history."
—Ernst Jünger

"As you proceed through life, following your own path, birds will shit on you. Don't bother to brush it off. Getting a comedic view of your situation gives you spiritual distance. Having a sense of humor saves you."
—Joseph Campbell

"Man cannot live without myth."
—Carl Jung

"The artist can only create what he is."
—Edred Thorsson

This is a new kind of book for me, but one that has deep roots and has been a long time coming. My occultism writings have always consisted of both poetry and prose, though it's fair to say my poetry has mainly been in the spotlight before. This is true even of my *Eagle's Mead*, where I have both poetry and essays, because two of its three essays are directly about poetry. But in this collection of nine occult essays, my prose gets the stage all to itself, and for once, I'm not writing directly about poetry in any of these essays. I have written poetry directly inspired by several of these essays (Eagle and Gar, Moldavite, Triadic Experiences, and Wewelsburg), but that poetry is collected in the companion volume to this one, *Shining Mead: Poems Inspired by Life, Conjunction, and Occultism*, which I encourage my readers to obtain as well.

In a way, this book is also an homage to Edred Thorsson / Stephen Flowers, since its format is inspired by his various "Rûna" volumes: *Green Rûna*, *Blue Rûna*, *Black Rûna*, and *Red Rûna*, which are collections of his essays on various esoteric topics. And as Edred made such essay collections, I've now done likewise in this volume with these nine essays. But unlike the essays in his volumes, which had mostly been previously published in various places, the nine essays in this volume have effectively never been released before, except to rather small and private audiences of about a dozen people or less. (Oddly, I've had remarkably little interest in getting others to publish my work outside of academia, and I have remained focused on self-publishing for my poetry and occult works.) And further unlike Edred's various *Rûna* books, I wrote all these essays with the intent that they would eventually be compiled into this book. Despite their range of topics, they fit together better than expected. As essays for occultists, they are not academic works (in the sense of a peer-review process, although the Wewelsburg essay comes closest), but they frequently draw on academic sources and embrace Polarian Method in starting with the known before moving into the unknown. In these last points, this book also has echoes of Edred's *Rûna* volumes.

These writings are all relatively recent. The Moldavite essay is the earliest of them, written in 2019, with seven more being written in 2022–2023, and the Wewelsburg essay last in 2025. In their esoteric natures, they are all informed by a synthesis of perspectives I've acquired as an initiate of the Rune-Gild and of the once-and-future Guild of the Grail. And these are reasonably mature perspectives, for I reached the critical 3° in both schools prior to writing any of these essays. Specifically, these degrees were Master in the Rune-Gild in August 2016 and Knight in the Guild of the Grail in June 2018. And the subject matter of all the essays is connected to concerns of either one or both of these schools. The Rune-Gild is reasonably well-known, and I dedicated my book *Eagle's Mead* to the Rune-Gild, so I won't go into further detail about my work in it. The Guild of the Grail, on the other hand, is all but completely obscure, so some words about it are needful, most especially since I've dedicated this volume to it, and because some of the essays herein are directly about it.

It is common for advanced initiates of occult schools to go outside the school where they got their start and work their way through the degrees of a different school. So after sufficient advancement in the Rune-Gild, I became one of those initiates. But what is surely exceptional in my case is that instead of joining some other living school (whether the Temple of Set, Dragon Rouge, the Hermetic Order of the Golden Dawn, the Ordo Templi Orientis, or something else), I started working with, in late 2013, the materials of an extremely short-lived order that had disbanded over a decade prior. That order called itself the Guild of the Grail, and I had at some prior point found the public version of its guidebook, *Liber Ars Collegium*. The guidebook proclaimed itself as "containing a description of the philosophy, organization, and methods of an Initiatic Order of Knighthood." I found it to have an inspiring and uplifting message, one that was centered around the symbolism of the Grail with a Solar orientation toward Transcendence and a Traditionalist viewpoint.

If you do magic hard enough for gaining initiatory development, the universe is likely to bring it to you, in whatever form is available under the circumstances and which suits your inclinations. It's fair to say I had been doing that around 2013. And so this strange path with the once-and-future Guild of the Grail came to me, rather than my working with some other already established order, or my founding a brand-new order. (The Odian Wandering and Triadic Experiences essays in this volume touch a bit more on what got me onto that path.) I was, after all, also pursuing something else at the same time that was just as important to my own initiatory development, namely grad school overseas. That was first through an MA/MPhil in Viking and Medieval Norse Studies at the Universities of Iceland and Oslo in 2014–2016, and subsequently a PhD in Icelandic Literature at the University of Iceland in 2017–2021. So perhaps my strange path with a dead order was the only one viable at the time with all that travel—and it also afforded me the opportunity to meet and work with one of the initiates of the original Guild of the Grail.

But getting back to the Guild of the Grail itself, its philosophical orientation and reading lists contained lots of material that is generally proscribed by the Western world's intelligentsia and professional-managerial class. They will insist that the material is inherently "problematic" in some fashion, which is certainly not the case. One can take it to a good place or a bad place. (I go into more detail on this in the Odian Wandering essay.) These include things like capital-T Traditionalism and the works of Julius Evola, René Guénon, and Oswald Spengler. So in good Odian Wandering fashion, this was a very transgressive quest in which to pursue the Grail. If the reader can manage to find that public guidebook in some dusty corner of the internet, he can decide for himself just how transgressive it actually is.

But due to the very short life of the Guild of the Grail (not much more than a year, if that), the reading list, the rites, and even its philosophy itself were all effectively untested beyond the Guild's creator, Sir Faustus. And nobody gets creating an order right on the first try. The successful ones all go through growth, development, and changes on their way to becoming well-established. Furthermore, at the time I started through the Guild of the Grail materials, I was already a Fellow (2°) in the Rune-Gild. That, of course, informed my perspective on those materials, especially the reading lists. Many of the books on those reading lists are compatible with a Rune-Gild perspective, but others of them are not. All of this is to say that I had to combine a certain amount of reconciliation and synthesis along with the growth and evolution of the material, and my "working edition" of the guidebook now has a number of differences from the original. My book *Eagle's Mead* was my Knighthood Work for the Guild of the Grail. In mysterious ways, it was indeed a manifestation of that reconciliation, synthesis, growth, and evolution. And now, the essays in this volume (all of them) are the further flowering of my development since then as both Rune-Master and Knight. Every tree is known by its fruit. Here's a brief rundown of the essays:

- **Odian Wandering Among the "Ettins"**: This is a statement of my commitment to free inquiry, intellectual independence, strange quests, and my rejection of the ideological extremism of today's intelligentsia and the professional-managerial class. It is partly magical autobiography.

- **Moldavite as the Stone and the Grail**: In the course of my Grail Quest, moldavite became my favorite gemstone, and that inspired me to write this essay that connects it to both the Grail and the Philosopher's Stone of the alchemists.

- **Eagle and Gar**: In this essay, I offer a new interpretation of certain aspects of Óðinn's hanging on the World Tree to win the Runes. My interpretation presents new ideas for using the Gar as a ritual tool today and perspectives for incorporating the symbol of the Eagle into the winning of the Runes.

- **The Canon of Nine**: That canon was the nine regal precepts of the Guild of the Grail, and the original materials simply stated them without providing any further description, commentary, or guidance on applying them. In this essay, I offer my interpretation and commentary on these precepts.

- **Towards a Meta-Order of Tradition**: In this essay, I discuss my conception of what the Guild of the Grail was aiming for, and what I consider its value and unique positioning as far as initiatory orders go, especially vis-à-vis Tradition.

- **The Quartets of the Elder Futhark and Anglo-Saxon Futhorc**: In this essay, I offer a speculative interpretation of the themes of each quartet of the Elder Futhark (and the corresponding quartets of the Anglo-Saxon Futhorc) that occultists may make use of in operative work.

- **The Fourth Ætt of the Anglo-Saxon Futhorc**: This is a direct continuation of the preceding essay, in which I offer a modern interpretation of how occultists today might approach and make use of that mysterious fourth ætt that the Anglo-Saxons added to their Futhorc.

- **Triadic Experiences for My Triple Quests**: Here, I talk about my initiatory path, with a focus on the kind of transformative, revelatory, mystical moments that the seeker may experience on the path, and hopefully contribute something to the understanding of the phenomenon by others. I also briefly touch on where my Quests may be going from here, namely with the American Futharch Runes, <americanfutharch.com>, for which much more is coming in the future. This one is also a magical autobiography.

- **Wewelsburg's So-Called "Black Sun" is Really Himmler's Round Table and Grail**: This is surely the crown jewel of this volume, its breakout "hit single," and the essay that has the best chance of making me infamous. And it is also far and away the longest essay of this volume at over 20,000 words. Vague and all-too-brief attempts have been made before to connect the infamous sun wheel design in the North Tower floor of Wewelsburg Castle to the Round Table and the Arthurian Mythos. But here, by the grace of the gods, I go the distance and present the ultimate apotheosis of that hypothesis. And it is the first truly complete explanation of that mysterious symbol that has ever been given, including an account of the sources that I believe were used in designing it and the purpose that Himmler intended for it. I've named the symbol the Round Table Sun Wheel, and on account of the significance of this essay, I've chosen it to grace the cover of this volume and to be a part of the book's title.

Read and enjoy with an open mind, in the spirit of Odian Wandering. If there is a unifying thread to all these essays, it is that they express a spiritual vision oriented toward Transcendence that's synthesized with Seeking the Mysteries. In any case, these essays are signposts to Spirit, just as my poetry is. They are also mile markers on my own road that makes a synthesis of the Mead, the Runes, and the Grails. It is a road that follows in the footsteps of Óðinn as a mythic exemplar and Drighten of the Mead, the Runes, and the Grails. May these essays show new vistas to initiates, magicians, occultists, esotericists, sages, heathen prophets, and other travelers of the hidden realms.

Eirik Westcoat
Winter Nights 2025

Odian Wandering Among the "Ettins": Support for Exploring Wherever the Adventure Leads

"It's very difficult to get a man to understand something when his salary depends on him not understanding it."
—Upton Sinclair

Opening Remarks
This essay is quite unlike the others that follow it. Yet it has here its proper place in this volume. It is various parts magical and intellectual autobiography, a response to my cancellation (past and future), advocacy for free inquiry, a condemnation of intellectual cowardice, a filter for the unworthy, and a catharsis. This essay is also a way of saying that I was in academia for its ideals, which are in conflict with its in-group mentality of saying and believing all the right things to fit in. Perhaps it and this volume will even get me cancelled from the few remaining academic publications I have left in the pipeline at press time? Finally, this essay is about my view of my own occult journey, and a way of saying that you cannot be a *great* occultist if you are a *safe* occultist. A number of other notable online occultists these days, such as Georgina Rose and Carolyn Lovewell, have gotten cancelled in recent years. And though the concept doesn't apply the same way to the older generation, it could be said that Stephen Flowers and Michael Aquino faced the equivalent of cancellation in their time. Perhaps it's an inevitable right of passage for the unsafe and advanced occultist. So now we begin with the great exemplar of unsafe and advanced occultists in the heathen tradition, Óðinn himself.

Odian Wandering in the Lore
It is well known that Óðinn seeks wisdom in the lore and pursues many avenues for it. I will recount some of that seeking here, focusing on those quests where he travels among ettins. Thus, I will not treat things like Óðinn's hanging on Yggdrasil, his use of his ravens, or his use of Mímir's head, as those wisdom-seeking

activities do not involve him dealing directly with ettins. Instead, most significant for my purposes are Óðinn's wisdom contest with Vafþrúðnir, his drink from Mímir's Well, and his Winning of the Poetic Mead. I will briefly discuss all three of them and their meaning.

The poem *Vafþrúðnismál* is the main source for Óðinn's wisdom contest with Vafþrúðnir. Óðinn, under the alias of Gagnráðr (He Who Advises Against), seeks out Vafþrúðnir in his hall, and after Óðinn demonstrates some cosmological knowledge, he and Vafþrúðnir wager their heads over who is wiser. In questioning Vafþrúðnir, Óðinn seeks knowledge of the past and present of the nine worlds before finally seeking knowledge of the future Ragnarök and bringing the contest to an end once he has learned what he wants to know.

In a different story, an ettin named Mímir guards a well located under one of the roots of Yggdrasil, and Mímir is very wise because he drinks from the well, which contains wisdom and intelligence.[1] Naturally, Óðinn is interested in getting some of this action, and so he asks Mímir for a drink. But Mímir demands a steep price, one of Óðinn's eyes. Óðinn agrees and gets a drink from the well, and his pledged eye remains in the well.

Finally, the last story concerns poetry. In it, the Mead of Poetry, made of the blood of the slain Kvasir (wisest of the gods), ends up in the possession of an ettin named Suttungr. As the mead would turn anyone who drinks it into a poet or scholar, Óðinn seeks it out. Under the alias of Bölverkr (Bale-Worker), he works for an ettin named Baugi for a summer (after facilitating the deaths of Baugi's nine slaves) in order to get access to the Mead. Then, after Baugi gets him into the mountain where it is stored, he spends three nights with the ettin-woman Gunnlöð, and then she allows him three sips of the Mead. Óðinn gulps it all down and escapes with it back to Asgard.

---

[1] There is also a Mímir who is clearly among the Æsir. Some consider this the only Mímir, and that he is both the guardian of the well and the severed head that Óðinn consults. The mythology is not absolute on this, and it can be read that there are two different Mímirs, which is the approach I take here.

Some common factors here should be noted. In all three quests, the ettins dwell outside of Asgard. In two of them, Óðinn hides his identity, presumably on the grounds that he would be quickly killed or otherwise thwarted by the ettins he is traveling among. This means he is traveling in hostile territory. As for Mímir's well, we are told it is near the frost-giants, but the territory, or at least Mímir, does not seem to be openly hostile, especially as it is likely that Mímir knows he is dealing with Óðinn. Also, the fact that Óðinn must give an eye shows that he values the drink greatly and that he is not in a position to force the drink from Mímir for a lesser price. All this shows that these ettins are indeed outsiders and not allied with Asgard in any way. In none of these quests are we told anything of what the rest of the Æsir thought of Óðinn going out of Asgard and dealing with these ettins. The one exception is that Frigg expresses concern for Óðinn's safety during his visit to Vafþrúðnir, which may be reflective of a general concern the Æsir have for Óðinn's safety in these quests. Regarding the Poetic Mead, it is clear the rest of the Æsir were in on it, because they put containers out in the courtyard for Óðinn to vomit the Mead into when they saw his return flight. Ultimately, the only reasonable conclusion is that the Æsir are supportive of Óðinn's quests, since he is throughout the mythology recognized as their lord, and these quests do not endanger his standing in the community of the gods, but rather they probably enhance it. That is, the Æsir recognize and appreciate the value of Óðinn's quests, even though he deals with the "enemy" or other dangers in doing so.

Applying Odian Wandering

Having discussed the lore regarding Odian wandering, it's time to turn to actual applications and concrete experiences of it. I take Óðinn-as-a-model-of-self-transformation quite seriously, and it has informed much of what I do. How does Odian wandering work? One part of this is the stanza, *Hávamál* 141, in which Óðinn says:

> Þá nam ek frævask
> ok fróðr vera
> ok vaxa ok vel hafask;

orð mér af orði
orðs leitaði,
verk mér af verki
verks leitaði.

Then I began to become fruitful and to be wise,
and to grow and to thrive;
a word got a word by a word for me,
a work got a work by a work for me.[2]

I've interpreted this elsewhere as a reference to robust productivity in composing poetry,[3] but it's just as applicable to anyone caught up pursuing interesting reading or research—one word will lead to another, and one book (work) will lead to another. To really be in the spirit of it, you do need to follow it wherever it leads, and then discover why it led you there. To be clear, I'm not advocating any abandonment of discernment. Discernment in evaluating what you find is of the highest importance. What you need to avoid is being a knee-jerk, closed-minded reactionary. That is, if the adventure leads you to reading a book by Julius Evola, by all means, be discerning in evaluating what Evola is saying and how it should be used. But don't go apoplectic and think "He was a horrible person, I won't read this, and nobody else should either" without even reading it. Indeed, I'm quite sure that nearly all of the people who go around condemning others for reading Evola have never actually read any Evola themselves and scarcely know the first thing about him. That, sadly, is the typical, unthinking, intelligentsia approach, and if that's you, then clearly you're not ready to follow the Odian path, and kindly please get out of the way of those who do. For those who are ready, when your Self is transformed, you will indeed find wisdom in the strangest places.

Is Odian Wandering Welcome Today?

Is today's academia and heathenry genuinely open to modern-day Odian figures who wander among the "ettins" seeking knowledge? It ought to be, but I think it has a long way to go if it truly wants

---

[2] *Eddukvæði* 1:350–52, and the translation is mine.

[3] Westcoat, "The Mysteries before Rune-Staves."

to emulate the lore. Yes, I read Evola, and in late 2018, admitted to liking one of his books. It went this way. I decided to participate in one of those Facebook chain memes, that of posting the covers of seven books you like, one per day with no other comment. On the fifth day, I posted the cover of Julius Evola's *The Mystery of the Grail*. Then the crap hit the fan and cancel culture came after me. Some of the perpetrators were even hoping to get me completely canceled out of the PhD program I was working in at the time. Fortunately, they did not succeed at that, and I went on to finish my fully funded PhD on time in 2021, although they did succeed in causing me a number of troubles. Such cancel culture has run off the rails in modern society, and has become a serious threat to labor rights and free speech—sacrificing labor rights and free speech to achieve "social justice" would be seriously counterproductive, and plays into the hands of capitalist bosses and aspiring totalitarians.[4]

In addition to Evola, I've read some of the other Traditionalist thinkers, chiefly Guénon, and some Traditionalist-adjacent ones, such as Spengler and Yockey. I read controversial things quite often, so I won't bother listing any more books or authors here, but follow the links in the works cited if you'd like to see some of the places I go for inspiration and new perspectives. To be clear, this is not an apology. I did nothing wrong, I'm not at all sorry for what I did, and I'll do it again. There are, however, moderate people out there with genuinely open minds who may be perplexed and truly want to understand why I would dare to believe in free inquiry and read Evola and certain other authors. This essay is for them.

In "inclusive" heathenry today, traveling outside the innangard and talking to the folkish, for whatever reason, is the sort of thing that will likely get you treated with great suspicion at a minimum. Indeed, given their level of concern with enemies and

---

[4] Ahmed, "Trying To Get Workers Fired," *Jacobin*, notes that "Firing people is neither an effective nor an ethical left-wing strategy in combating racism." Phillips, "The Threat to Civil Liberties," *Jacobin*, notes the horrid situation of how many people have quite wrongly "come to view the defense of free speech as something foreign to the Left and a weapon of oppression."

"fascists," I really can't envision them tolerating Odian figures who are seeking wisdom in the modern-day equivalents of Jötunheim—whatever we may postulate as Jötunheim, whether it is the folkish, certain books, anything outside of what is approved by the intelligentsia or professional-managerial class, or something else on somebody's official or unofficial list of enemies. For instance, I've no doubt there are "inclusive" heathens who have begun to regard me poorly for some of the strange places my reading and writing have gone, and they'll probably consider this very essay and the book it is in as further confirmation that I'm a heretic. All of that (both in general and in particular to me) is extremely unfortunate—though many of them advocate for Loki and his deviant qualities, it seems as if they are not comfortable with Óðinn. It is a curious case where it seems as if they would welcome Loki and exclude Óðinn. That this is the worst of the four possible permutations of welcoming/excluding applied to the pair Loki/Óðinn—it effectively means embracing chaos while simultaneously rejecting wisdom—should not require any further comment. Regarding Óðinn's quests, we see that the wisdom and power gained from them is enormous, and that the boons they bring to Asgard are no less than the ultimately positive outcomes that result from some of Loki's impulsive behaviors. And today's advocates of Loki will be quick to remind you of those, of how Loki's chaos brings about renewal and prevents a stagnated culture. Genuine Odian wandering does the same thing—brings about renewal and prevents stagnation—and it frequently does it with way less trauma to the innangard.

I rather get the impression that the folkish heathens are more tolerant of their people wandering among the "ettins," regardless of whatever else might be said about their other kinds of tolerance. Because I have never gotten the impression that any folkish heathens I've met were ideological inquisitors—a claim I wish I could make about the inclusives. To make a temporary detour that will have relevance later, I note the following. Namely, inclusive and folkish heathenry each have certain good qualities, and I desire a heathenry that is the best of both, rather than being forced to choose from an artificial ideological binary. And one of my defining characteristics (maybe it comes from autism?) is my general push-back against various artificial binaries.[5] Ultimately, I am something other than an inclusive or folkish heathen. I am instead a secret third thing, and my god Óðinn is a god of secret third things.

But there is at least one organization that is not merely in favor of such Odian wandering; it's founded upon it. That would be the Rune-Gild. I've been a member of it since 2011, and a Master since 2016. The Gild expressly views Óðinn as an exemplary model of self-transformation, and Óðinn's many quests, whether among ettins or not, are a part of that model, and one that seekers should apply in their own lives. That is just one of many reasons why I love this particular school and have found the best community for me in it. One finds *genuine* tolerance and community in it, not a sham of internal witch-hunting that's covered up with a veneer of ostentatious virtue signaling. Indeed, I think its broad-mindedness and affirmation of free inquiry and Odian questing are a significant cause of its tolerance and community, as such allows and encourages the members to find value in their differences without needing to erase their diversity.

Transmuting My Christian Heritage

To get on with the details, my reading of Traditionalists helped me to deal with my Christian heritage. And that is one of the most important things I have gotten out of them, most specifically Evola. Although the numbers are increasing, very few Westerners today are born and raised in a heathen religious perspective. Many still come from a Christian background in their families. But even those who are raised in heathen or godless households cannot escape some level of Christian influence in the surrounding culture. Anyone who converts to heathenry must ultimately come to terms with his Christian heritage on both the personal and cultural level, one way or another. In my case, I was raised in what was a nominally Christian household. My mother was the main

---

[5] In the United States, one may think of our two-party system of the Democratic vs. Republican parties. I'm like the man in Ernst Jünger's *The Forest Passage* who votes "no." See "Review: *The Forest Passage* by Ernst Jünger," *The Postil Magazine*.

churchgoer of the family, being United Methodist throughout my youth. My father seems to have a general belief in the Christian deity, but he had little use for church attendance except at major holidays (and only in my youth, probably at the instigation of my mother). And so it was generally just my mom who took me and my brother to church on many Sundays. In hindsight, I must reckon the United Methodist Church to be a fairly middle-of-the-road faith in the America of the 1980s—it had no extreme elements to it whatsoever. It probably functioned largely as a social cohesive, or at least it used to. Where I grew up, it seemed as if every small town had its own United Methodist Church.

Around the time I was fourteen years old, a different sort of religious impulse arose in me, although I am not sure where it came from. In any event, I wanted a more serious faith. Somehow, I ran across some Christian Fundamentalist magazines (yes, magazines were still a thing in the early 1990s), and it briefly lured me in. I won't try to recount all the details, as it was a rather dark time for me. The short version is that I became utterly convinced I was doomed to absolute non-existence in the Christian afterlife.[6] This made me quite depressed and nearly suicidal rather than drag things out longer. But before I could get to the point of planning how to go through with it, something suddenly snapped in my mind, and this terrible mental knot of dysfunctional belief was instantly cast out. I don't know why it happened, but suddenly, I no longer believed I was doomed to non-existence, nor did I believe much of anything about an afterlife, Christian or otherwise, at that point. Thus began my years as what I like to call "apagnosticism"—a combination of the words apathy and agnosticism, summed up in the flippant attitude toward religious matters of "don't know and don't care." A fringe benefit of the experience is that it served as an inoculation against suicidal thoughts, and that immunization still remains highly effective

---

[6] It's a mistake to think that all Christian sects believe in an eternity in hell for unrepentant sinners. This particular fundamentalist sect, which I think was obsessed with the Book of Revelation, had the belief that the sinners would be cast into the lake of fire on Judgment Day and simply cease to exist after that.

even after thirty years. I would occasionally still struggle with depression, but never again would I think of taking my own life. Although I freed myself from Christian tyranny in the sense of having religious fealty to it, my heritage and the culture around me remained unchanged.

Nevertheless, the religious impulse in me was not destroyed, and it would not slumber forever. It would reemerge a bit over eight years later, in 1999 when I was twenty-two and discovered a pagan path that ultimately led me to embrace heathenry in 2004 when I was twenty-seven, but that journey does not need to be recounted here. In the course of my heathenry, I would nonetheless reflect on the fact that the culture around me was at least nominally Christian, and that my ancestors, going back at least a thousand years, were all Christians also. For all I know, maybe some were even in the Knights Templar. And here I am, repudiating all of that heritage by choosing to forsake the Christian deities and return to Óðinn and the other Gods of the North. Yet somewhere in my life, I picked up a general tendency against suppressing, cutting off, or denying aspects of myself. I felt a need to do something with all this Christian heritage and my own past Christianity, rather than just throwing it away completely in the trash. Some heathens, perhaps, can just throw it away. Others must find their own way of dealing with it, which will be different for each individual.

Evola and the Guild of the Grail

My personal way of dealing with my Christian baggage came through a particularly fascinating and obscure bit of esotericism. Sometime around 2006, give or take, I had stumbled across the public guidebook of a then-defunct Initiatic Order of Knighthood called the Guild of the Grail (which had been founded in 2001, but disbanded around late 2002).[7] I found its spiritual message to be rather inspiring, although I did not do much with it as my level of initiatory development was non-existent at that time. But it stuck with me in the back of my mind. Fast forward to Autumn 2013. At that point, I was a Fellow in the Rune-Gild and the Grail

---

[7] That public guidebook may still be on the internet somewhere.

was exerting a pull on me, and I undertook and completed an esoteric poetry project called "Runes for the Grails."[8] This triggered my Grail Experience, and after that, I was sufficiently inspired to follow the initiatory path laid out in that Guild of the Grail guidebook, to the point of reaching its Knighthood on its terms.[9] I completed this quest in June 2018, and my book *Eagle's Mead* is my Knighthood Work in that quest.

What was the Guild of the Grail? It aimed to create a modern Western esoteric initiatory Order with a Traditionalist approach based on the works of Evola and Guénon (roughly one-sixth of the level one readings are by those two authors), and centered around the symbolism of the Grail. Apropos the main thrust of this essay, its reading lists included more controversial works and authors than just those two. And today's intelligentsia typically feels threatened by anything Traditionalist with a capital-T. But there are indeed valuable insights and spiritual perspectives to be found there. I mean that in a general sense, as well as a personal one, but I won't attempt to enumerate all of that here. In short, the Guild of the Grail, Traditionalism, and Evola's interpretation of the Grail were the pieces I needed to alchemically transmute my Christian heritage. They allowed me to see Christianity as an overlay upon the Grail Mythos, not the true originator of the Grail Mythos. By embracing Evola's perspective—which saw the Grail as ultimately a Hyperborean mystery, not a Christian mystery—I could transmute my Christian heritage by seeking the perennial Tradition behind it. And I saw that the Grail Tradition, partaking of a solar universalism that is superior and anterior to much of medieval Christianity (and thus not tainted by Christianity's fallen nature vis-à-vis solar religions), held everything that was genuinely valuable for me in Christianity, and so I was able to leave the rest of Christianity behind. And so I would remove the Christian trappings of the Grail Mythos (which is the most rich and fascinating post-pagan mythology to come out of Europe, bar

---

[8] The full project is written up as an essay and poem. Eirik Westcoat, "Runes for the Grails," 249–89, 178–82.

[9] See the essay, "Triadic Experiences for my Triple Quests," elsewhere in this volume for more on my Grail Experience.

none) in order to embrace the pagan roots of the Grail Mythos. In effect, this was what I already did in inspirational fashion with my "Runes for the Grails" project. But it was my later reading of Evola and my Guild of the Grail Work that enabled the larger work to be completed and integrated in my being. Other fruits of that quest include several of the essays in this volume. Those fruits not only come from the gold that I find in these strange and controversial places, but also from the fact that my mind is daring and curious enough to look there. The intelligentsia, being trapped in the dogmas they owe allegiance to, lack the imagination to discover and create the things that I will.

And so that was how I turned my Christian heritage from an albatross around my neck into a source of power and inspiration fully compatible with my heathen and transcendent spiritual vision—one in which I view myself (in part) esoterically as a Heathen Grail Knight in the legacy of the Knights Templar. Some of my readers may find this inherently contradictory, but that's the point. This quest led me to a place of power where that's not contradictory. It's okay if you don't want to go to that particular place. Maybe you don't need to. Other seekers aiming to deal with their Christian heritage may find different paths that don't involve Evola or other writers that get you cancelled by the intelligentsia for reading them. And good for those seekers. In any event, as long as one's approach does not harm others, I'm not going to judge people for whatever means they use to transmute their Christian heritage on a pagan path. I'd love it if everyone extended me the same consideration, but I've already accrued enemies among those who won't extend such a courtesy.

What about the Whataboutism? Countering the Sophists

Now is the time to deal with the whataboutism of my intelligentsia enemies. In short, they aren't seeing clearly when they condemn me (or anyone else) for merely reading Evola and baselessly assume that I must be "alt-right" for liking some of his books. In many or even most cases, they are probably engaging in some sort of repression/projection dynamic.

In a page from *Existential Comics*, the tendency for Nietzsche's ideas to be misunderstood by small-minded adolescents is rightly mocked.[10] Undoubtedly, a similar comic could be made for Evola, except that Evola is less well-known. And it is certainly true that there are right-wingers who take Evola's material and other things, such as the so-called "Black Sun," Hyperborea, the Knights Templar, and so forth, to a bad place. But this is no less true of the intelligentsia and left-wing types who go apoplectic in response to that material, such as those who have attacked me—after all, how could they attack me unless they have already taken the material to a bad place themselves? I have been called to a different path, to take these things to a good place, a place of Spirit, and I have chosen to heed that call.

But for those left-wingers, Evola's actual thoughts and writings are irrelevant. Instead, they see a liking for Evola as merely an "identity marker" for their "far-right" "enemy." My brain (perhaps due to autism?) doesn't construct my identity in that fashion (in terms of choosing between different packages of identity markers).[11] My primary identity, to the extent that I actually have one, is spiritual-vocational (something that I believe is adequately revealed in my poetry and esoteric prose). Matters of race, ethnicity, gender, and the general mess of things that constitute "identity" to today's extremists (on both ends of the spectrum) simply do not interest me. As I mentioned earlier, I generally don't go for the artificial ideological binaries on offer in today's world of identity, and my detractors can't tolerate this. Here, one of the big ones is fascist vs. anti-fascist.[12] There is also racist vs. anti-racist.[13] Again, I am a secret third thing on both

---

[10] "Nietzsche Returns," *Existential Comics*.

[11] See, for instance, this fascinating piece on an identity theory of autism. After I read it, the actions of neurotypicals (and my academic enemies) made much more sense to me. Vance, "The Identity Theory of Autism," *NeuroClastic*.

[12] On this binary, see Tuccille, "Choose Sides? You Bet," *Reason*, which leads off by noting that "Advocates of liberal society are a side in themselves, and the left- and right-wing thugs battling in the streets are rival siblings from an illiberal family."

[13] On this binary, see Pluckrose and Lindsay, "How to Be Not-Racist," *New Discourses*.

counts there. Those two binaries go a long way to proving a particular point from one of my favorite bloggers: "The opposite of one bad idea is usually another bad idea."[14]

And I've gradually come to realize that I'm extremely unlike my detractors, and the numerous people who lose their heads over Evola. I'm reading Evola for spiritual, religious, and esoteric ideas, not political or racial ones. And also not in any attempt to "signal" my "identity" to people who identify as "fascist." But I've become aware enough to understand how the left-wingers are treating things (as just mentioned, as mere identity markers in identity group struggles) and to get annoyed by it, because it's a nuisance (for instance, getting canceled caused me a lot of trouble). That is, they have certain obsessions about identity and how it is constructed, and they project that onto me, and they're completely unable to see that I don't construct my identity the same way they do. And yes, I do blame them for this blind spot in their supposedly "rational" analysis of things around them. Especially the academics, because they should know better, since their profession is supposed to value clear and rational inquiry, and it's disgusting to see them fall into an unreflective, knee-jerk attitude whenever anything remotely "right-wing" is mentioned.

Partly this may be because many of these left-wingers are atheistic. Thus, they deny the existence of anything spiritual and have a giant blind spot toward spiritual things. And since they themselves don't believe in religion and spirituality, they assume other people don't either, and so they try to explain away the religious and spiritual impulse as something else. The result is that they are unable to believe or understand that I genuinely am reading Evola out of spiritual motivation. An earlier generation of these atheistic academics resorted to Marxism and tried to explain everything in terms of economic class struggle. A fair chunk of the current generation tries to explain everything in terms of identity group conflicts. Undoubtedly, this fad too will pass, and the next generation will come up with something equally faddish. In the end, spirituality will have to be understood *qua* spirituality, acknowledging it on its own terms, and by not trying to explain it

---

[14] Greer, "The One Drop Fallacy," *Ecosophia*.

away or reduce or deconstruct it so that it can be comprehended to fit within the prejudices, bigotries, and latest fads of the intelligentsia.

However, this essay isn't meant to convince my enemies, although it would be nice if it did. Regarding cancel culture, an anonymous friend said: "For those who are determined to be offended and outraged, there is no compromise that will be sufficient, because they are driven by a desire to be outraged. However, while they are noisy, there are far fewer of them than they like to think." Some of my enemies are indeed the sort "who are determined to be offended and outraged." And better writers than myself, such as John Michael Greer, have written on the massive present-day failings of the intelligentsia (he prefers to refer to the professional-managerial class—the terms are not precisely the same, but they certainly have a great deal of overlap), and those writers have not woken the intelligentsia from their hate and bigotry.

I'll take another perspective here on Evola before concluding this section. In the movie *The Empire Strikes Back*, Luke asks Yoda what is in a certain cave that he's been told to go into, and Yoda replies with "only what you take with you." There's a lot more to Evola than what people take with them, of course, but to me, it often seems that's all many people find in Evola. On the left, you have people who want to be outraged looking at Evola; on the right, you have people looking to justify their prejudices who are reading Evola. Both tend to find only what they take with them. The belligerent loudness of the former and the hateful applications of the latter only serve to make it that much more difficult to find the genuine gold that is there. I'm neither of those, and so I find something different when I read Evola—hopefully it is some of the gold. Of course, there are other clear-headed people on both ends of the spectrum who are reading Evola, but they are not quite as loud as the rabid dogs. As for Evola having some really questionable writings, I don't doubt it, although I haven't read all of his books yet. But people find spiritual value in the Bible, and it's filled with lots of atrocious stuff. And yet the Bible doesn't get nearly as much opprobrium.

Another Example: The Millerman School

I'm certainly not the only person out there attempting to explore strange corners that the intelligentsia would like to deem off-limits. Michael Millerman, a recent University of Toronto PhD in Political Science, started his own online teaching after finding the doors of academia shut to him for daring to inquire into certain controversial philosophers, such as Heidegger and Dugin, for the value they may hold. This material from an earlier version of his website makes his case that there is value to be found among them, and it's critically important:

> Michael completed his PhD in Political Science at the University of Toronto in 2018, researching a question that had been on his mind since his undergraduate days: what is the relationship between such philosophical fields as metaphysics and ontology, on one hand, and our understanding of politics, on the other?
>
> A few years into pursuing this question, Michael discovered that access to the issue was blocked by a historical circumstance: 20th-century political philosophy, rightfully aghast at the horrific consequences of Nazi ideology, had, perhaps too hastily, made a strong taboo against studying any of the philosophers typically associated, directly or indirectly, rightly or wrongly, with that movement.
>
> The reasons for instituting such a taboo are clear and understandable. But, motivated by his question, Michael began to notice that the zealous defence of liberalism came at a cost: **philosophical teachings incompatible with liberalism** *but not for that reason either untrue or unhelpful* **were forgotten or suppressed**. Thus the spectrum of political philosophy was artificially constrained, possibly keeping important discoveries at bay.[15]

I generally agree with Millerman's view of how political philosophy (and I would extend it to the rest of philosophy in general) has gotten stuck in a cul-de-sac in the post-war period

---

[15] Millerman, *Millerman School*, website accessed October 2022. Emphasis in original.

and that important discoveries are being precluded.[16] To extend a metaphor, I would say that the "zealous defense of liberalism" he refers to is not merely throwing out the baby with the bathwater, but has advanced to the sacrifice of babies in order to prevent the existence of bathwater. That fanaticism seems strange and misplaced when one considers communism. As an ideology, communism has a much higher body count than fascism, and it spread farther over the world than just Europe, and yet no one has gone absolutist on making sure to purge every last drop of that particular bathwater, and, what's more, the world hasn't come to an end out of a failure to do so.

More can be illuminated on the "bathwater" issue by looking at some examples, starting with the Western intelligentsia's attitude toward Heidegger, which comes out of his connections to the Nazi party in the WWII era. It can be pointed out that Heidegger's works are being translated into Hebrew and published in Israel.[17] It is perhaps comparable to Douglas P and his musical project Death in June, notorious for his use of controversial imagery in his music, stage shows, and album art: one of his concerts was shut down by Antifa in the United States, but he has played shows in Israel without incident. I will add a third, final example. Edred Thorsson's book *Hermetic Magic* was published by Weiser in 1995. Before that, he had first pitched it to Llewellyn, but one of the internal reader reports accused it of being "Aryan Hermetic Magic" and racist, and so the book was rejected.[18] There is, of course, nothing racist about the book, as anyone who's read it can

---

[16] The Millerman example is from philosophy, but undoubtedly it applies to other fields as well. For instance, there are surely scientific realms where the "conventional wisdom" keeps people from exploring and thereby stymies new discoveries.

[17] Ilany, "Why It's Futile to Boycott Top Nazi Philosopher Martin Heidegger," *Haaretz*. The subtitle remark is "Heidegger's philosophy is experiencing a renaissance among Israelis while being attacked in Germany, his birthplace." Haaretz is, of course, an Israeli Jewish publication. For an excellent, nuanced take on Heidegger's importance, see Miller and Millerman, "The Heidegger Question," *IM—1776*.

[18] Edred Thorsson, *History of the Rune-Gild*, 50–51.

easily see—it was a case of that internal reader projecting his prejudices upon Edred and the text. And Edred himself points out that the book was based mostly on German-Jewish scholarship. You can guess where I'm going with this: *Hermetic Magic* was also later translated into Hebrew and published in Israel! I have no doubt that numerous other examples could be found. But I think these three are enough to suggest that the Western intelligentsia has a pathological streak in it, in this regard. If the Israelis clearly don't obsess over the "ideological bathwater" like the Western intelligentsia does, why, exactly, should anyone take the Western intelligentsia seriously on this matter?

I would seem to be on a comparable path in my esotericism, in exploring things that liberalism has attempted to preclude out of an excessive and fanatical defense of itself. But Millerman has stated the problem here with striking clarity, more so than I could have managed. And he hints at what I think is the real root of the matter: a liberalism that is incredibly insecure with itself, despite its dominance over the Western world today. I can't have any respect for a liberalism that is wallowing in excessive fear. It is as said in a translation of *Völsunga saga*: "No one can advise you, if you are afraid of everything. You are not like your kin in courage."[19] Today's liberalism is indeed afraid of everything, and not like its kin of earlier centuries in the courage to enjoy free inquiry and vigorous debate and a wide variety of ideas, and we should look upon it in disgust until it grows a backbone again. One might also characterize it as a case of a ruling elite that comes off as being elephants who are afraid of mice. And so there really ought to be a robust discussion of those "philosophical teachings incompatible with liberalism but not for that reason either untrue or unhelpful." Otherwise, it makes it seem that liberalism is a fragile ideology that lives in fear of boogeymen, and so turns to repressive tactics and abandons the commitments to freedom that it was supposedly founded upon.

---

[19] Byock, *The Saga of the Volsungs*, 63.

A Short Recap

It's time to bring this discussion to a close and recap the major points. Odian wandering and the free inquiry it requires are good things in the lore and the world. On its presence in the lore, the following five points are primary:

1. Free inquiry is supported by the lore in the stories of Óðinn's wanderings.
2. The outsiders that Óðinn wanders among are genuine outsiders and allowed to simply be outsiders. That is, moral judgments are not made upon them.
3. That wandering brings great benefit to the Æsir.
4. The Æsir, as a properly functioning society, are supportive of that wandering.
5. That the high god of the pantheon does this wandering demonstrates the high value that the societies with this mythology placed upon it.

As for the presence in today's world, such Odian wandering among the "ettins" can be defended as producing real, positive value in at least the following three ways:

1. It can lead to individual growth and transformation (my personal story).
2. It can lead to new insights to be communicated at an interpersonal level (my other essays in this volume).
3. It can bring benefits to the wider humanities and society (Millerman's story).

I have also addressed the enemies of Odian wandering and identified their criticisms of it to be illegitimate in the following five ways:

1. They resort to condemning free inquiry because they became trapped in bubble-think.
2. They contradict themselves, that while they make a big show of being inclusive, they are nonetheless still afraid of outsiders.
3. They are more often than not projecting their own prejudices and bigotries on free thinkers.
4. Their fanaticism toward merely reading controversial thinkers is an overblown reaction, especially when compared to a people with more "skin in the game."

5. Fear of free inquiry is a sign of cowardice that is unbecoming of a proper intelligentsia.

To be absolutely clear, I am a staunch supporter of free inquiry, and nobody should be called a fascist just because of the books he reads or the people he chooses to talk to and learn from. Accusations of "fascism" should be limited to clear and overt words and actions. Hunting for crypto-fascists by attempting to split hairs, read tea leaves, and conjecture over guilt-by-association, ambiguous online content, or other writings (as was done to me) is a wholly illegitimate enterprise, and the people who do that sort of thing should be met with the harshest condemnation.

Final Remarks

This was a strange essay for me to write, for it is quite unlike the others in this volume. But it Needed to be written, because mine is a path of free inquiry in seeking wisdom. And in the modern world, there is increasing hostility to free inquiry. Having been the target of some of this hostility, I chose to stand up for myself and my quest here, and it is also directed toward any future hostility that might come my way.

I'm sure there are people who could read this essay, and, in spite of everything, still accuse me of being a fascist. I have two final things to say about that. The first is to remind them of Mussolini's own statement on fascism: "Fascism should more properly be called corporatism, since it is the merger of state and corporate power." I'll be blunt: in today's America, there is already way too much of both state and corporate power, and there is likely nothing that could be a more terrible idea than merging them. The second is to quote my favorite blogger, because he has said it far better than I could:

> And if, dear reader, your response to the above is to accuse me of being a fascist—the standard response of the Ctrl-Left these days to even the mildest disagreement—let me ask you this. We both know what the word "fascist" means, and it doesn't mean

individual liberty, representative democracy, and a lack of enthusiasm for invading other countries.[20]

If anyone is still claiming I'm a fascist, it says plenty about them and nothing about me. Such people need to get over themselves. For the rest of you, the fruits of Odian Wandering are ahead.

Works Cited

Ahmed, Bilal Zenab. "Trying To Get Workers Fired Is the Wrong Way To Fight Racism." *Jacobin*. October 4, 2020. <jacobin.com/2020/10/fired-workers-racism-social-media>.

Byock, Jesse, trans. *The Saga of the Volsungs*. Berkeley: University of California Press, 1990.

Eddukvæði. Edited by Jónas Kristjánsson and Vésteinn Ólason. 2 vols. Reykjavík: Hið íslenzka fornritafélag, 2014.

Edred Thorsson. *History of the Rune-Gild: The Reawakening of the Gild 1980–2018*. North Augusta, SC: Arcana Europa, 2019.

Greer, John Michael. "The Alt-Right, the Ctrl-Left, and the Esc-Center." *Ecosophia*. July 4, 2018. <ecosophia.net/the-alt-right-the-ctrl-left-and-the-esc-center/>.

Greer, John Michael. "The One Drop Fallacy." *Ecosophia*. November 15, 2017. <ecosophia.net/one-drop-fallacy/>.

Ilany, Ofri. "Why It's Futile to Boycott Top Nazi Philosopher Martin Heidegger." *Haaretz*. September 16, 2017. <haaretz.com/opinion/2017-09-16/ty-article/.premium/why-its-futile-to-boycott-this-top-nazi-philosopher/0000017f-e034-d3a5-af7f-f2be5c850000>.

Jünger, Ernst. *The Forest Passage*. Translated by Thomas Friese. Telos Press Publishing, 2013.

---

[20] Greer, "The Alt-Right, the Ctrl-Left, and the Esc-Center," *Ecosophia*. I should clarify that I find constitutional monarchy to be an acceptable form of representative democracy, and one that has some advantages over the American kind, but I recognize the impossibility of America ever having monarchy on any level. In such an America, the concept of monarchy is most useful to individuals from an internal, self-development perspective. See also my essay "The Canon of Nine" elsewhere in this volume.

Miller, Daniel, and Michael Millerman. "The Heidegger Question." *IM—1776*. April 25, 2023. <im1776.com/2023/04/25/the-heidegger-question/>.

Millerman, Michael. *Millerman School*. Accessed October 2022. <millerman.teachable.com/>.

"Nietzsche Returns." *Existential Comics*. January 10, 2022. <existentialcomics.com/comic/428>.

Phillips, Leigh. "The Threat to Civil Liberties Goes Way Beyond 'Cancel Culture.'" *Jacobin*. July 12, 2020. <jacobin.com/2020/07/cancel-culture-harpers-letter-free-speech>.

Pluckrose, Helen, and James Lindsay. "How to Be Not-Racist." *New Discourses*. October 23, 2020. <newdiscourses.com/2020/10/how-to-be-not-racist/>.

"Review: *The Forest Passage* by Ernst Jünger." *The Postil Magazine*. November 1, 2018. <thepostil.com/review-the-forest-passage-by-ernst-junger/>.

Tuccille, J. D. "Choose Sides? You Bet. But Antifa and Fascism Are the Same Side." *Reason*. August 22, 2017. <reason.com/2017/08/22/choose-sides-you-bet-but-antifa-and-fasc/>.

Vance, Terra. "The Identity Theory of Autism: How Autistic Identity Is Experienced Differently." *NeuroClastic*. October 17, 2021. <neuroclastic.com/the-identity-theory-of-autism-how-autistic-identity-is-experienced-differently/>.

Westcoat, Eirik. "The Mysteries before Rune-Staves: Explaining Futhark Order and Rune Names via an Ur-Poem Prior to Runic Writing." Forthcoming.

Westcoat, Eirik. "Runes for the Grails: Creating Old English Rune Poem Stanzas for Cweorð, Calc, Stān, and Gār." In *Eagle's Mead*, 249–89, 178–82 (poem translation). Long Branch, PA: Skaldic Eagle Press, 2019.

Moldavite as the Stone and the Grail

Introduction

In popular culture, the Grail is most famous as a cup, supposedly the one that Jesus drank from at the Last Supper, and which was then subsequently used to catch his blood while he was on the cross the next day. It is indeed such a cup or dish in many of the Grail romances. Yet in the best and greatest of the Grail romances (especially for those who have a Traditionalist point of view), Wolfram's *Parzival*, the Grail is most clearly and definitely a *stone*. With good reason, many before me have connected the Stone of the Grail to a particular green gemstone of at least partially extraterrestrial origin known as moldavite. In this essay, I will affirm that connection and go a bit further. I will also connect it to the specific approach to the alchemist's stone discussed by VandenBroeck and Schwaller de Lubicz, providing a new lead for hermeticists to work with. Then I will discuss some practical possibilities for esoteric work that may be tried with moldavite, using Wolfram's tale as a guide. Finally, I will move into some more speculative territory by discussing innovative esoteric applications that combine Wolfram's tale with Norse mythology.

Why Gemstones?

Some readers might be aware of the New Age fascination with the magical properties of gemstones and may even be thinking: "Isn't that all a bunch of hokum?" Only from a very limited, chronocentric perspective. While it is certainly true that an appreciation of the magical properties of gemstones currently seems to be monopolized by the New Age movement, it wasn't always that way—such an appreciation of gemstones has Traditional roots. G. Ronald Murphy has quite a lot to say about the gemstones that feature in *Parzival*, and this is just the start:

> The importance of the gemstone is to be found everywhere in Wolfram. He not only identifies the Grail as a precious stone but also uses stones to mark the inner structure of his work by identifying its two foci: first, the progress of his hero toward feeling the compassion necessary for 'owning' the Grail, and

second, the suffering of the community on Mount Salvation as they faithfully await the healing of Anfortas.[1]

During the height of the Middle Ages, gemstones had a vibrant and accepted place in the Christian tradition:

> They enjoy a status almost as a natural sacrament, a gift instituted by the Creator "in the beginning" to do good, capable of bringing about what their color signifies to the poetic mind. . . . In the thirteenth century, the belief in their effectiveness was a point accepted by scholars and priests, abbesses and monks, lay men and women of all classes, learned and unlearned alike. Medieval Christianity had the testimony not only of pagan antiquity but also of enthusiastic and competent Christian contemporaries, such as Bishop Marbode and Abbess Hildegard of Bingen—*teste David cum Sybilla*—to support its belief in the powers of gems. The two wrote extensively on the specific "virtues" of each type of gem, and when an occasional unimaginative rationalist voice had the temerity to object, there was trouble. . . . Why would the medieval church so unequivocally embrace and defend what appears to be merely the secular natural science and traditional folk medicine of its day? The answer is that the premier theologian of late antiquity and the theologian most influential in the Middle Ages, St. Augustine of Hippo (354–430 AD), had located gems in the theological world as a very exceptional gift of God, as resident in the overflow of the rivers of Eden, pure and untainted holdovers from the Garden of Paradise.[2]

Thus, it would certainly be a valid enterprise to revalorize gemstones in today's world from a Traditionalist perspective. Murphy's book, *Gemstone of Paradise*, and especially its second chapter, "The World of Precious Stones," is an essential starting point for those who want to explore medieval gem lore as it relates to *Parzival*.

Moldavite: Exoteric Properties

Before taking a closer look at the Grail Mythos, it's time to introduce this mysterious gemstone that is worthy of connection

---

[1] Murphy, *Gemstone of Paradise*, 41.

[2] Murphy, *Gemstone of Paradise*, 42.

to the Grail. The general scientific consensus is that moldavite (*vltavín* in the Czech region where they are found) is a gemstone within the class of natural glasses known as tektites, which are formed by meteorite impacts. Significant about tektites is their near-zero water content (less than 0.02%), which is notable compared to obsidian, a natural glass that contains about 2% water. Moldavite is virtually alone among the tektites in having the most brilliant, rich, green color, whereas the others are usually dull and black. At this time, it is also the only confirmed European tektite. About 14.7 million years ago, the entire world's supply of moldavite was formed by a meteorite impact in Ries near Stuttgart, Germany.[3] The impact released an enormous amount of energy, many times that of the most powerful atomic bombs, and liquified a lot of silica material—silicon dioxide, or common sand, mixed with various trace elements—a great fusion of Earth and Fire. Blasted way into the sky, this molten material rained down over great distances, cooling and hardening as it fell. What is found today is primarily what landed in certain regions in the current-day Czech Republic. Perhaps 275 tons of it has survived to the present day, and roughly 300–500 thousand pieces of it have been found so far. The scientific characterization of moldavite first occurred in the eighteenth century; however, since pieces were made into Neolithic-era tools, it is clear that humans have been using the stone for a long time prior to the modern era. Before this eighteenth-century distinction was made, it was common to call any clear green stone an "emerald," although such a designation is now reserved for crystals of the mineral beryl.

Moldavite, like other tektites, will always have inclusions—there are no "perfect" pieces. The two main types of inclusion are typically tiny bubbles and fiber-like lechatelierite, often requiring magnification to see. Their presence is essential for distinguishing genuine moldavites from synthetic fakes (which are generally just

---

[3] The case on moldavite origins is not completely closed as there are a number of mysteries and peculiarities that remain, especially when compared to the other tektites. See Wells, *The Moldavite Enigma*, for a theory that postulates a much older origin, although it seems rather far-fetched.

ordinary colored glass, but which attain some sophistication at times). Spectroscopy can also distinguish genuine moldavites, which will have certain trace elements, from the synthetics, which lack them.[4]

The rough stone typically has a peculiar texture, and certain varieties, Besednice in particular, are highly valued in their uncut form for their "spiky-hedgehog" appearance. However, moldavites are sometimes cut, faceted, and polished into gemstones, suitable for setting into jewelry. The material is also suitable for carving, and finely-detailed artistic pieces, called glyptics, can be made from it, some of which will carve the entire surface, others of which will use the natural rough texture to complement or complete the carving. To illustrate these possibilities, the following photos are of three pieces of moldavite from my personal collection: an eagle-head glyptic (27.65 carats), a rough stone (59.70 carats), and an oval-cut gemstone (22.30 carats):[5]

Another peculiar property, found in only a small percentage of moldavites, is a unique sound effect that is produced when they are clinked against other moldavites or glass. The ones that make this sound are known as "angel chimes."[6] Finally, I would note that moldavites are generally recognized as precious stones, and they become increasingly expensive with size, and certain varieties, such as the Besednice, are extremely pricey.

---

[4] The source of much of the technical information in most of these two paragraphs is Hanus, *Moldavite*, 11–37.

[5] For these photos, my thanks go to InnerVision Crystals, the online store where I purchased these stones. They are not to the same scale.

[6] One can easily find online videos that demonstrate the differing sounds from ordinary moldavite and "angel chime" moldavite, and the latter is indeed quite special and worthy of the name.

The Grail Stone According to Wolfram and Others

Now it is time to see how the Grail Mythos can be connected to moldavite. Wolfram's direct statement on the Grail is worth quoting at length, and is quite unequivocal about the Grail being a stone, as well as some of its most important properties:

> They [those who dwell with the Grail at Munsalvæsche] live by a stone whose nature is most pure. If you know nothing of it, it shall be named to you here: it is called *lapsit exillis*. By that stone's power the phoenix burns away, turning to ashes, yet those ashes bring it back to life. Thus the phoenix sheds its moulting plumage and thereafter gives off so much bright radiance that it becomes as beautiful as before. Moreover, never was a man in such pain but from that day he beholds the stone, he cannot die in the week that follows immediately after. Nor will his complexion ever decline. He will be averred to have such colour as he possessed when he saw the stone—whether it be maid or man—as when his best season commenced. If that person saw the stone for two hundred years, his hair would never turn grey. Such power does the stone bestow upon man that his flesh and bone immediately acquire youth. That stone is also called the Grail.
>
> Today a message will appear upon it, for therein lies its highest power. Today is Good Friday, and therefore they can confidently expect a dove to wing its way from Heaven. To that stone it will take a small white wafer. On that stone it will leave it. The dove is translucently white. It will make its retreat back to Heaven. Always, every Good Friday, it takes the wafer to that stone, as I tell you; by this the stone receives everything good that bears scent on this earth by way of drink and food, as if it were the perfection of Paradise—I mean, all that this earth is capable of bringing forth. Furthermore, the stone is to grant them whatever game lives beneath the sky, whether it flies or runs or swims. To that knightly brotherhood the Grail's power gives such provender.
>
> As for those who are summoned to the Grail, hear how they are made known. At one end of the stone an epitaph of characters around it tells the name and lineage of whoever is to make the blissful journey to that place. Whether it relates to maidens or boys, no-one has any need to erase that script. As soon as they have read the name, it disappears before their eyes. As children they arrived in its presence, all those who are now full-grown

there. Hail to the mother who bore the child that is destined to serve there! Poor and rich alike rejoice if their child is summoned there, if they are to send him to that host. They are fetched from many lands. Against sinful disgrace they are guarded for evermore, and their reward will be good in Heaven. When life perishes for them here, perfection will be granted them there.[7]

The type of stone or its color is never mentioned by Wolfram, but it is carried on a green cushion or carpet. The Grail's origin is implied to be heavenly when Flegetanis says of it that: "A host abandoned it upon the earth, flying up, high above the stars."[8] However, for more of a direct statement of the Grail's heavenly origin, we must turn to the *Wartburgkrieg*, where in strophe 143 it says:

> Shall I then bring the crown
> that was made by 60,000 angels?
> Who wished to force God out of the Kingdom of Heaven.
> See! Lucifer, there he is!
> If there are still master-priests,
> Then you know well that I am singing the truth.
> Saint Michael saw God's anger, plagued by this insolence.
> He took (Lucifer's) crown from his head,
> In such a way that a stone jumped out of it,
> Which on earth became Parsifal's stone.
> The stone which sprang out of it,
> He found it, he who has struggled for honor at such high cost.[9]

This only leaves the question of why the Grail Stone is commonly said to be green or an emerald. I cannot seem to find where this may have come from, but it is quite a widespread view today. Perhaps it is an emergent, upwelling truth, a case of spontaneous manifestation of genuine Tradition? In any case, Evola notes it as an emerald, but does not clarify an ultimate source when he says:

---

[7] Wolfram, *Parzival and Titurel*, 198 (Book IX, §469–71).

[8] Wolfram, *Parzival and Titurel*, 192 (Book IX, §454).

[9] Simrock, *Der Wartburgkrieg*, 176–77. This is an edition of the medieval Codex Manesse, Janaer Leiderhandschrift, along with a German translation. The English translation here is from Pinkham, *Guardians of the Holy Grail*, 46.

According to others, the stone that fell to earth was an emerald that adorned Lucifer's forehead. It was cut into the shape of a bowl by a faithful angel, and thus the Grail was born. It was given to Adam before he was expelled from the Garden of Eden. Seth, Adam's son, having temporarily returned to the earthly paradise, took the Grail along with him. Other people transported the Grail to Montsegur, a fortress in the Pyrenees, which Lucifer's armies besieged in order to get the Grail back and put it into their leader's crown, out of which it had fallen; but the Grail was allegedly saved by knights who hid it within a mountain.[10]

However, we need not make too much fuss over identifying a source, as there is only one remarkable gemstone found in Europe that can be said to come from the heavens, and it is indeed moldavite, which, as noted above, is green and was commonly referred to as an emerald before being properly distinguished.

The Alchemical Stone According to VandenBroeck

So, what does any of this have to do with alchemy and the Philosopher's Stone? Potentially quite a lot, if one follows the approach of a particular adept, André VandenBroeck, as I do here.[11] He starts with the three major alchemical principles: Sulphur, Mercury, Salt. Next are the four classical elements: Earth, Air, Fire, Water. Finally, there come four particular qualities that occur in two opposing pairs: hot/cold and dry/humid.[12] He organizes them together in a triangular matrix in the following diagram:[13]

---

[10] Evola, *The Mystery of the Grail*, 71.

[11] My explication and summary here of his views is based on VandenBroeck, *Al-Kemi*, 109–36 (chapter 5), and my readers are greatly encouraged to explore the details of his thoughts there. It's certainly a major part of the book, as demonstrated by the illustrations—there are six total in the center of the book, three of them pertain to this matter in that chapter, and one of them is cited below.

[12] The latter pair will be of note to those who observe the distinction between the dry, magical path and the humid, mystical path.

[13] The illustration is VandenBroeck, *Al-Kemi*, Plate 3. Plate 4 in the book expands the system with other aspects, such as colors and senses.

Occult Mead

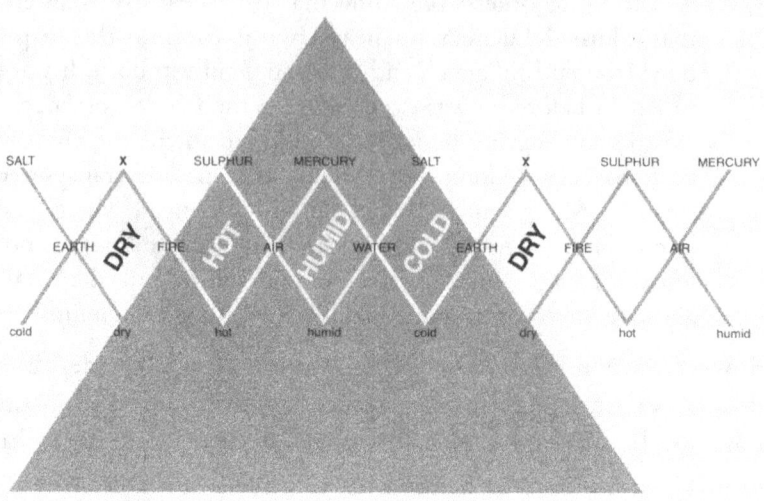

One sees that Sulphur is thus a product of Fire and Air and has an inherently "hot" nature. Mercury is then a humid expression of Air and Water, and Salt is a cold expression of Water and Earth. VandenBroeck expresses the desire to run the diagram further in either direction:

> We cannot help but feel that the cold dryness of Earth yearns for the dry Fire which would close the cycle of our diagram in a new principal entity....
>
> Nature cannot recombine the dryness of fire with the dryness of earth. The very impasse implies an opportunity for a step nature is unable to take, a step beyond nature. It is the Promethean act, the intelligent manipulation of "divine thievery," the godly flight into the sun, and the successful return. It is also the alchemical *Grand Oeuvre* in one of its aspects, the dry way of the crucible whose sign is the Cross.[14]

That is, we want a principle X that is a dry expression of Earth and Fire. R. A. Schwaller de Lubicz had something to say about this diagram and ideas that VandenBroeck presented to him:

> In fact, our first principle in the next octave would not be Sulphur at all, which is a combination of Fire and Air, but a

---

[14] VandenBroeck, *Al-Kemi*, 119. Attributed to VandenBroeck.

principle whose nature combines Fire and Earth. Well, there is no such principle in nature, according to this physics; there is no principle X, as you put it in your diagram. Note that I said: in nature! Would it help you to know that your X principle could be considered a fair description of what adepts call: the stone?[15]

At this point, VandenBroeck complains that substituting "stone" for "X" is no help, since to him at the time, he did not know what was meant by "stone" and it was just substituting one unknown for another. Then Schwaller de Lubicz sheds some more light on the matter:

> I hope you don't visualize the philosopher's stone as a rock or other mineral body to be locked up in a cupboard when not in use. The stone includes the gesture that handles it, that makes it happen; its identity as stone exists only in the manipulation; at other times it is that most common and valueless substance the books always talk about as being found anywhere. I call your X principle "stone" because the dryness, the milieu of dryness comes into being and the stone *is* dryness, as Salt is cold, Mercury humidity, Sulphur heat. And that dryness which is new to the natural octave, will now act on the natural salt with the power of that X principle, and the work it must accomplish is precisely the work one would ask of the stone, which has a dryness never attained by natural salt: the stone is going to dry the salt in order to effect the next octave.[16]

Here, of course, the stone is the *magnum opus* of alchemy, the philosopher's stone capable of turning base metals into gold. VandenBroeck's discussion then turns to other matters and does not offer any identification for the stone. However, there is enough here for me to be so bold as to proceed further and suggest a symbolic identity for the stone, and by now, the astute reader can probably guess where I'm going to end up with this.

The Stone Revealed?

Now, what would fit VandenBroeck and Schwaller de Lubicz's specifications? What substance is dryness, with a hot-cold tension,

---

[15] VandenBroeck, *Al-Kemi*, 129. Attributed to Schwaller de Lubicz.

[16] VandenBroeck, *Al-Kemi*, 130. Attributed to Schwaller de Lubicz.

and yet a combination of Earth and Fire, and, at the same time, (usually) "that most common and valueless substance," especially when it is not in use as the Stone?

Glass. Yes, ordinary glass. It is made largely from silicon dioxide, and a common form of that on the Earth's surface is ordinary sand. Silicon dioxide and related silicate minerals make up 90% of the Earth's crust, so it could scarcely be more common than that. And thus sand is a worthy symbol of the element of Earth. And what is one simple way to make glass? By melting sand —that is, applying Fire to it. Typically, glass is also fairly dry, having a low water content. And both sand and glass are usually quite valueless. But ordinary glass is missing something. It's a completely terrestrial phenomenon, and generally nature-bound, even the volcanic glasses. Can a symbol of the non-natural, of Fire from the Heavens, be brought into this? Yes, via the tektites, glasses made from Earth combined with Heavenly Fire as discussed above, and which are even lower in water content than the volcanic glasses. So really, any tektite might thus be acceptable as a symbol of the Stone, and I would add there are indeed several other tektite species on Earth, which might be investigated for some esoteric purposes in this regard (although that is beyond the scope here). But given the location of the Grail Mythos in Europe and its connection with a green stone that fell from the heavens, only one tektite is suited to be both the Stone and the Grail at the same time: moldavite. From this, especially given the prior confusion of emerald and moldavite, we should also consider another appropriate connection as a possibility, namely that the "emerald" of the Emerald Tablet (*Tabula Smaragdina*) of Hermes Trismegistus—a legendary repository of alchemical wisdom—was actually a moldavite.

Alchemical Implications

It is clear that VandenBroeck and Schwaller de Lubicz are talking about alchemy as a laboratory art, in addition to being an occult activity. As I am not an alchemist, I cannot go further with any laboratory implications of this, including whether or not a special kind of glass is even a reasonable identification of the Stone for practicing alchemists. The alchemists out there are invited to try practical experiments with it, however. Nevertheless, my comments here should be taken as mainly pertaining to the symbolic aspects of moldavite vis-à-vis the Stone.

As de Lubicz is reported to have said above, the Stone is not the Stone when sitting on the shelf outside of the time of a manipulation, and so strictly speaking, neither is moldavite. However, there is a peculiar parallel between moldavite as the Stone and the nature of a human being to be pointed out here. I see moldavite's combination of the natural with the non-natural, specifically heavenly fire, as mythologically analogous to human beings themselves. Two mythologies in particular come to mind (there may be others). First is the Greek, in which Prometheus stole fire from the gods and gave it to humans. Less obvious is the story in Norse mythology, in which the divine triad of Óðinn-Vili-Vé endowed a pair of trees (natural forms) with special gifts (non-natural qualities, including *óðr* (inspiration), which may be seen as a metaphorical Fire) to make human beings. It can readily be seen that many humans do not use their fire or special gifts to the fullest, at least not most of the time. Only during special states or with special training does this occur. In other words, for most of us, the something special "exists only in the manipulation." That would be a certain raised quality of our consciousness—at other times, our "consciousness" is a rather common and valueless substance.

Here I will leave the alchemical remarks, hoping to have shown that moldavite is useful as a superior symbol of the Stone, as it has qualities symbolic of a non-natural origin, and though made largely of glass, it is far from common and valueless. So it is perhaps the best symbol to be found among the gemstones of planet Earth, and occupying such a place, it is worthy of being our Grail Stone.

Moldavite: General Esoteric Properties

Now it is time to consider some esoteric properties of moldavite. As it was only distinguished in the last few hundred years, there are no very old sources for this material.[17] The books by Hanus, Wells, and Simmons & Warner in the works cited feature the best material that I'm familiar with, and they are all reasonably level-headed books that recognize a need to integrate both science and esotericism when dealing with moldavite.[18] There is general agreement that moldavite is an excellent stone, perhaps the best, for promoting the transformation and evolution of one's consciousness to higher levels—for making the Ascent. It is even thought to produce a spontaneous kick-start in spiritual development in some individuals—an echo of how Wolfram's Grail calls people to serve it. It is also thought to be a solar stone with an affinity for gold, the heart, and healing. It is thought to be an aid to meditation, especially when in physical contact with the wearer. Unlike quartz, for instance, moldavite does not retain negative imprints. That is, the stone can be "charged" with sunlight, but it cannot absorb negativity from nasty people handling it—this kind of purity makes good sense considering its identification with the Grail Stone. Perhaps most peculiar, it is thought that individual stones may each have their individual personalities and variations in properties. Also, that it is easier to sense the "energy" of moldavite than that of any other stone, even for the most inexperienced and unintuitive people. I am certainly not the most psychically sensitive person, but I've felt the energy of this stone, and continue to feel quite drawn to it. So much so that for me, among minerals, moldavite is the Stone, and everything else is just rocks, and though I have occasionally fancied collecting stones before, moldavite is the first stone that I've ever spent significant money on.

---

[17] It would be an interesting, but long, project to try to tease out the qualities of moldavite from those of other green stones that medieval authors would have confused it with, and I will not attempt it here. The *Mineralium* of Albertus Magnus would be one starting point for that.

[18] Note, however, that their esoteric materials should still be taken with some amount of discrimination. This goes especially so for the "channeled" material, which can be rather dubious at times, to say the least.

General Possibilities for Esoteric Work

Obviously, one can use moldavite to represent the Grail Stone in rituals, but here I'll go beyond that. Having identified it with the Grail Stone, we can try making practical esoteric use of moldavite for the purposes described by Wolfram in *Parzival*. First, in *Parzival* it is said that only the baptized can see the stone. I take this as a metaphor that one must have taken a significant preliminary step toward connection with Spirit in order to unlock the potential of moldavite. From the mention that messages appear on it, one might try scrying with it to obtain messages in letters or in the esoteric alphabet of your choice—my own work would use runes. Given the particular mentions by Wolfram of how the Grail identifies those who are to serve it and who is to be the proper wife for the Grail King, seeking out esoteric fellow travelers and ideal lovers could also be tried with the stone. Relatedly, one could meditate on it as the Emerald Tablet in seeking alchemical wisdom directly from Spirit. The annual arrival of a dove placing a host upon the Grail is a metaphor for its connection directly to Spirit and its power being renewed by Spirit. So moldavite can be thought of as having such a connection as well. Nevertheless, one could try boosting this effect by enacting a rite designed to celebrate this connection—charging with sunlight would be the simplest way, but more elaborate invocations designed to call down renewed power from the heavens could also be designed. From the phoenix connection, one can use the stone in initiatory rites of death and rebirth. Its description as a preserver of life and youth makes it suited for thaumaturgy that aims to preserve and maintain the good things that one has in one's life—generally, the peak of one's existence, which would include health, conditions, and possessions. Aiming transpersonally to the highest possibility, we can extend that to preserving and strengthening the influence of Spirit and Tradition upon the world—this is, after all, the supreme purpose of the Grail in Wolfram's *Parzival*. Finally, the metaphor of the Grail providing food and drink means that this stone can help us obtain spiritual nourishment to sustain us.

Speculative Old Norse Possibilities for Esoteric Work

Now I move into an even more creative realm. One of my own special works is bringing the Grail Mythos into the Germanic Heathen Tradition. I began this with my ground-breaking essay, "Runes for the Grails: Creating Old English Rune Poem Stanzas for Cweorð, Calc, Stān, and Gār."[19] The latter three of these are the final three runes of the Anglo-Saxon Futhorc at its maximum of 33 runes. Edred Thorsson connected these final three to some of the Grail Hallows: the Cup, the Stone, and the Spear, respectively.[20] Out of that material, I will only focus on the Stone here. As Edred suggested identifying the Cup and the Spear with Óðrœrir (the poetic mead) and Gungnir (Óðinn's own spear), respectively, I extended that by equating the Stone with the most significant stone in Norse mythology, Hrungnir's heart. Hrungnir was a rock giant who was defeated by Thor in a duel, and Snorri considered it important enough to tell us about his special heart:

> Hrungnir had a heart that is renowned, made of solid stone and spiky with three points just like the symbol for carving called Hrungnir's heart has ever since been made.[21]

This spiky shape may be what is called the valknut today. That is not the only possibility, but it's the one I use. As for the kind of stone that Hrungnir's heart is made of, there is nothing in the Old Norse lore for identifying that. So we must speculate and experiment. My scholarly research into the valknut identified Hrungnir's heart, and thus the valknut shape, as the exemplary steady heart of the brave warrior (which is contrasted to the quivering heart of the coward),[22] making it an excellent symbol for a new Germanic Heathen Knighthood. Taking the imaginative leap of treating that heart as made of moldavite suggests another magical use for the stone: increasing one's courage and strengthening one's heart.

---

[19] Westcoat, *Eagle's Mead*, 249–89.

[20] Edred, *ALU*, 205–08.

[21] Snorri, *Edda*, 78.

[22] Westcoat, "The Valknut: Heart of the Slain?"

Another more tenuous possibility may be considered. In Norse mythology, Mímir's head (after it was cut off from his body) was preserved by Óðinn through the use of herbs and spells, so that it would not rot. It then speaks to Óðinn of hidden things. It is a stretch to identify Mímir's head with the Grail Stone, but the head has become immortal and unchanging, so in a sense, it has become stone-like. So one could try using a suitable moldavite as a "Mímir's head" and scrying with it in that fashion, to receive clairaudient messages, as opposed to the more clearly sanctioned written messages of the Grail Mythos.

Conclusion

Over the centuries, many have looked to the Grail Mythos and sought to find an actual physical Grail in the world. With this short essay, I hope to have illuminated some intriguing aspects and possibilities pertaining to my favorite candidate for a physical Grail: moldavite. Unlike the physical implements of the crucifixion, which would necessarily be singular and unique, this particular Grail, though it may have originated in a singular event, exists in a multitude of small pieces. Thus, any true seeker can get a piece and connect with this special legacy of Spirit. Of course, just getting one of these stones is only the start of the journey—there are many mysteries to seek in it, many possibilities to explore, and much Work to be done. Ascent!

Works Cited

Edred Thorsson. *ALU: An Advanced Guide to Operative Runology.* San Francisco: Weiser, 2012.

Evola, Julius. *The Mystery of the Grail: Initiation and Magic in the Quest of the Spirit.* Translated by Guido Stucco. Rochester, VT: Inner Traditions, 1996.

Hanus, Radek, et al. *Moldavite: Mysterious Tears from Heaven.* Czech Republic: Granit Publishing, 2015.

InnerVision Crystals. <www.innervisioncrystals.net>.

Murphy, G. Ronald. *Gemstone of Paradise: The Holy Grail in Wolfram's Parzival.* Oxford: Oxford University Press, 2006.

Pinkham, Mark Amaru. *Guardians of the Holy Grail.* Kempton, IL: Adventures Unlimited Press, 2004.

Simmons, Robert and Kathy Warner. *Moldavite: Starborn Stone of Transformation*. East Montpelier, VT: Heaven and Earth Publishing, 1988.

Simrock, Karl. *Der Wartburgkrieg*. Stuttgart and Augsburg: J. G. Cotta, 1858.

Snorri Sturluson. *Edda*. Translated by Anthony Faulkes. London: Everyman, 1995.

VandenBroeck, André. *Al-Kemi: Hermetic, Occult, Political, and Private Aspects of R. A. Schwaller de Lubicz*. Hudson, NY: Lindisfarne Press, 1987.

Wells, Jr., K.B. *The Moldavite Enigma: Unlocking the Alchemic Secrets of the Moldavite Effect*. Tempe, AZ: Original Falcon Press, 2008.

Westcoat, Eirik. *Eagle's Mead: Initiatory Poetry and Prose*. Long Branch, PA: Skaldic Eagle Press, 2019.

Westcoat, Eirik. "The Valknut: Heart of the Slain?" *Odroerir: The Heathen Journal* 3.2 (November 2015): 1–23.

Wolfram von Eschenbach. *Parzival and Titurel*. Translated by Cyril Edwards. Oxford: Oxford University Press, 2006.

Eagle and Gar: Enhancing One's Rune-Work with These Powerful Symbols

Introduction
In the quest for the Runes, Óðinn is our supreme exemplar. And so one must begin with the most important lore of the Rune Quest, which is the section of *Hávamál* known as the Rúnatal, stanzas 138–45. There is much written about all of these stanzas as a guide to Rune-Work, but the basis of my discussion here will be the beginning, stanzas 138–39:

> Veit ek at ek hekk
> vindga meiði á
> nætr allar níu,
> geiri undaðr
> ok gefinn Óðni,
> sjálfr sjálfum mér,
> á þeim meiði
> er manngi veit
> hvers hann af rótum renn.
>
> Við hleifi mik sældu
> né við hornigi;
> nýsta ek niðr,
> nam ek upp rúnar,
> œpandi nam,
> fell ek aptr þaðan.
>
> I known that I hung
> on a windy tree,
> nights all nine,
> wounded by the gar,
> given to Óðinn,
> myself to myself,
> on that tree,
> of which no man knoweth
> from what roots it rises.
>
> They dealt me no bread
> nor drinking horn,
> I looked down;
> I took up the Runes

roaring I took them,
and fell back again.[1]

It is generally agreed that here, Óðinn is hanging on the World Tree, Yggdrasil, in working his runic self-initiation. Yggdrasil contains the nine worlds of existence, but it also contains a number of animals, which include a serpent (Níðhöggr) among the roots, a squirrel, four harts, and—most importantly for my purposes here—an eagle sitting at the top. The symbolism of these animals is much debated, but what has not been discussed, to the best of my knowledge, is their connection—if any—to Óðinn's runic initiation. Of course, the lore does not mention any role for them, so one must draw on a variety of appropriate sources in piecing together a well-reasoned speculation for such a role. On the other hand, a ritual tool—the gar—is the only ritual tool explicitly used in connection with Óðinn hanging on the World Tree, so no argument is needed for why it is important to examine. Nevertheless, it has not received any special attention as a ritual tool or a specific symbol of focus for Rune-Work according to the Rune-Gild's curriculum, the *Nine Doors of Midgard*. Nor, it should be added, has it apparently received any special focus outside the Rune-Gild either. In this essay, I will discuss how the symbols of the Eagle and the Gar can give us new ways to think about and focus our Rune-Work, and in the case of the Gar, a new ritual tool to use. I begin with the Eagle.

The Eagle

Óðinn hangs on the World Tree, and it is common to interpret the initiation as resulting in Óðinn's death and return to life. There is an eagle at the top of the World Tree, and in skaldic kennings, it is common for eagles to be considered carrion birds. My revolutionary perspective here is to consider that the Eagle feeds on Óðinn's corpse between his death and rebirth, and what that implies.[2]

---

[1] *Eddukvæði*, 1:350; Edred, *The Nine Doors of Midgard*, 3.

[2] As a point of emphasis, I will capitalize Eagle when I refer to the Eagle sitting at the top of the World Tree.

Eagle and Gar

Let us first consider the sources for the Eagle. *Grímnismál* 32 mentions the presence of an eagle, Ratatoskr, and Níðhöggr, in the World Tree, characterizing the first as above and the last as below, but that is all:

> Ratatoskr heitir íkorni
> er renna skal
> at aski Yggdrasils;
> arnar orð
> hann skal ofan bera
> ok segja Níðhöggvi niðr.
>
> Ratatosk is the squirrel's name,
> who must scurry
> about on Yggdrasill's ash;
> the eagle's utterance
> he must bring from above
> and tell to Nidhogg below.[3]

The lack of a name for the Eagle here, where names are given for the other two, seems rather telling: it either does not have a name, or the name is being deliberately hidden. This is quite peculiar, as there are a downright excessive number of names for just about everything but the Eagle in *Grímnismál*: halls of the gods, rivers, valkyries, Óðinn, and more. Snorri, in *Gylfaginning*, is probably drawing on knowledge of *Grímnismál* when he says the following, where he manages to add some small details, but not the name of the Eagle:

> Örn einn sitr í limum asksins, ok er hann margs vitandi, en í milli augna honum sitr haukr sá er heitir Veðrfölnir. Íkorni sá er heitir Ratatoskr renn upp ok niðr eptir askinum ok berr öfundarorð milli arnarins ok Níðhöggs.
>
> There is an eagle [that] sits in the branches of the ash, and it has knowledge of many things, and between its eyes sits a hawk called Vedrfolnir. A squirrel called Ratasok runs up and down through the ash and carries malicious messages between the eagle and Nidhogg.[4]

---

[3] *Eddukvæði*, 1:374; Larrington, *The Poetic Edda*, 53.
[4] Snorri, *Edda: Prologue and Gylfaginning*, 18; Snorri, *Edda*, trans. Faulkes, 18–19. Bracketed text in original.

This Eagle has much knowledge, yet there are no reports of Óðinn ever consulting it. That a hawk sits between its eyes is a curious detail, but one which I will not address here. However, I will return to the matter of the nameless Eagle and Óðinn's failure to consult it later.

One of the famous named eagles in the lore is Hræsvelgr, whose name means Corpse-Swallower.[5] He is known from the question-and-answer sequence in *Vafþrúðnismál* 36–37:

> *Óðinn kvað:*
> „Segðu þat it níunda,
> alls þik svinnan kveða
> ok þú, Vafþrúðnir, vitir,
> hvaðan vindr um kømr,
> svá at ferr vág yfir;
> æ menn hann sjálfan um sjá."
>
> *Vafþrúðnir kvað:*
> „Hræsvelgr heitir,
> er stir á himins enda,
> jötunn í arnar ham;
> af hans vængjum
> kveða vind koma
> alla menn yfir."
>
> *Odin said:*
> 'Tell me this ninth thing,
> since you are said to be wise,
> and you, Vafthrudnir, know,
> where the wind comes from
> which blows over the waves,
> which men never see itself.'
>
> *Vafthrudnir said:*
> 'Carrion-swallower he is called,
> who sits at heaven's end,
> a giant in eagle's shape;
> from his winds, they say,
> the wind blows
> over all men.'[6]

---

[5] Lindow, *Norse Mythology*, 181–82.
[6] *Eddukvæði*, 1:362; Larrington, *The Poetic Edda*, 42–43.

Is he equivalent to the Eagle that sits on top of the World Tree? Maybe, but Snorri does not make the equation, even though he mentions both in *Edda* separately. Also, the two source poems, *Vafþrúðnismál* and *Grímnismál*, give no particular cause to think they are the same. I will say they are not the same: Hræsvelgr is clearly called a giant (*jötunn*) in this, and I will argue for a different identification for the *Grímnismál* Eagle.

I will note only two more eagles from *Edda* here, both from the story of the winning of the Poetic Mead. When Óðinn has just finished gulping down all of the Poetic Mead and goes to make his escape, the following takes place:

> Þá brásk [Óðinn] í arnarham ok flaug sem ákafast. En er Suttungr sá flug arnarins, tók hann sér arnarham ok flaug eptir honum.
>
> Then [Óðinn] turned himself into the form of an eagle and flew as hard as he could. And when Suttung saw the eagle's flight he got his own eagle shape and flew after him.[7]

There is a notable difference here between these two eagles. Óðinn is able to transform himself into an eagle and has the power to do this intrinsically, but Suttungr (a giant) has to put on an eagle shape and cannot do this on his own without help, much like how Loki is said to borrow a falcon shape from Freyja when going to visit the giants. From where did Óðinn get the power to transform into an eagle? That is never specified in the lore, but one possible interpretation is that consuming the Poetic Mead gave him this power. That is not the only possibility, however. But it is time to turn to other evidence about eagles in Old Norse lore.

The Gripsholm Runestone (Sö 179) is one of a great many runestones raised to commemorate the fateful expedition by Yngvarr víðförli (the far-traveled) to the Caspian Sea. Many Vikings died on it, and few returned, yet it inspired more runestones than any other Swedish event. This stone contains some notable poetry in *fornyrðislag* meter in honor of Yngvarr and his brother Haraldr:

---

[7] Snorri, *Edda: Skáldskaparmál*, 1:4–5; Snorri, *Edda*, trans. Faulkes, 63–64.

> ÞæiR foru drængila, fiarri at gulli, auk austarla ærni gafu. Dou sunnarla, a Særklandi.
>
> They went manfully, far after gold, and in the east gave [food] to the eagle. They died in the south in Serkland.[8]

To give food to the eagle is a metaphor in skaldic poetry that means "to kill enemies (and leave them for eagles to eat)." In addition to that runestone, the metaphor is found in several poems, and there it is very clearly about killing enemies as well. Corpses slain in battle are "food of the eagle," "the delicacies of the eagle," and "the eagle's barley," in poems by Einarr Skúlason, Ketill hœngr, and Þjóðólfr Arnórsson, respectively. But it should be asked whether the poets were really thinking of Óðinn when they said they fed the eagle. Although not directly stated, that is extremely likely. It is clear that the skalds were indeed thinking of Óðinn frequently in reference to corpses, because many kennings can be seen that use the names of Óðinn's ravens or wolves: Huginn, Munin, Geri, and Freki. There is even a direct Óðinn reference with a well-known *heiti*: "Yggr's falcon-barley." All of those corpse kennings and others may be found in the database of the Skaldic Project.[9]

Interestingly enough, none of those corpse kennings ever uses a proper noun for an eagle—that is, all of their eagles are nameless. Feeding Óðinn's named animals is undoubtedly a way of honoring the All-Father by offering the battle-slain to them, and thus him. As for the nameless eagles, their mention may be a dedication of the slain to Óðinn in his guise as Arnhöfði (Eagle-Head). The Germanic tradition of human sacrifices to Óðinn goes back a long time—Tacitus specifically mentions such sacrifices to him (giving his name as Mercury in the standard *Interpretatio Romano* of the time).[10] In the later saga material, the literature indeed mentions dedicating slain enemies to Óðinn specifically. One example may be found in a legendary saga where King Heiðrekr dedicates the enemies he has slain in battle to Óðinn.[11]

---

[8] Barnes, *Runes: A Handbook*, 77–78. Bracketed text in original.
[9] *Skaldic Project*, Kennings, "corpse, slain."
[10] Tacitus, *The Agricola and the Germania*, 108 (ch. 9).
[11] Tolkien, *The Saga of King Heidrek the Wise*, 26.

Now all this information must be put together. I argue that we should see the nameless Eagle of the World Tree and the skaldic kennings as none other than Óðinn himself! This would indeed explain why the Eagle is nameless in *Grímnismál* and elsewhere—the poets, who are naturally followers of Óðinn, know this well enough, and the Initiated in their audiences surely recognize it too, so it is kept as a secret in plain sight. And this is why Óðinn never seeks out the Eagle, despite Snorri calling it very knowledgeable, because they are one and the same. But the Eagle is not exactly the ordinary Óðinn—it is Óðinn's higher self or wode-self.[12] When Óðinn hangs on the World Tree to gain the Runes, wounded by a spear, he is giving food to his own higher self, the Eagle in the World Tree that consumes his corpse. And so when he takes up the runes roaring, his whole essence has been transferred into the Eagle—he has become the Eagle, and he roars as the Eagle in triumph. His falling back afterwards indicates that he has reconstituted his usual body anew to return to work in the manifest realms. As the Eagle is Óðinn, the other eagles—Hræsvelgr and Suttungr—are definitely not Óðinn, since they are both giants with an eagle's shape. It is Óðinn alone who has the power to transform into an eagle on his own, having won this through his runic initiation. When Óðinn changes into an eagle to escape with the Poetic Mead, it is not a newly acquired power, but I think it likely that the Mead offers him great assistance in the transformation in this instance. The skaldic poets honored this identity of Óðinn and Eagle through their metaphors: as Óðinn fed the Eagle of the World Tree, the warriors they commemorated in verse were said to feed eagles, since the Eagle was Óðinn, receiving the sacrifice of a human being. However, it was Odinists who worshipped Óðinn by offering him corpses through either the religious cult or through slaughter on the battlefield. But the Odian[13] with Initiated knowledge aims to emulate Óðinn, not

---

[12] "Wode-self" refers to a Rune-Gild approach to the notion of a higher self; see Edred, *The Nine Doors of Midgard*, 161–65, 180–81.

[13] The distinction here between Odinist (one who worships Óðinn) and Odian (one who emulates Óðinn) also originates in the Rune-Gild; for more on the distinction, see Edred, *The Nine Doors of Midgard*, vii–xi.

worship him. Therefore, he seeks to give food to his eagle within, to his own higher self, just as Óðinn did. This is no call for us to become soldiers and kill in battle—your lower self is the only acceptable food for the eagle within. Nor is it a call for a literal suicide on a physical tree—your higher self does not have a physical form to consume your flesh. Instead, it is a call to the inner work, to hang on your Yggdrasil within through Rune-Work and thereby feed your lower self to your eagle within, so that you can roar as the eagle when taking up the Runes. The Runer reading this now has a powerful new metaphor to guide his work and a new way to appreciate one of the most important lines in the entire Hávamál—*sjálfr sjálfum mér*!

The Gar

Now it is time to consider the supreme ritual tool of Óðinn's runic initiation, the spear, which appears in *Hávamál* 138 as the word *geirr*. It is cognate to Old English *gār*, which is given as the name of the final rune of the Anglo-Saxon Futhorc in the only surviving manuscript transcript of the Old English Rune Poem (although *Gār* does not have a strophe in the poem). For his esoteric system of Triadic Rune-Names, Edred gives the names of the seventh rune as Proto-Germanic **gēbō*, **galgōn*, and **gaizaz* (gift, gallows, and spear),[14] showing that he considers Óðinn's runic initiation and the spear to be central to the meaning of this rune. This **gaizaz* is the Proto-Germanic source of the later words *geirr* and *gār*. The material that could be connected to the gar is voluminous, and there is more out there than what will be covered here. Here, I aim to cover the material about the spear that most particularly pertains to its symbolic powers, especially those useful in an initiatory setting.

Óðinn is very much identified with his spear. Óðinn is called *geirs dróttinn* (lord of the spear) in stanza 22 of Egill Skallagrímsson's *Sonatorrek*.[15] It is well known that Óðinn has a spear named Gungnir, forged for him by dwarves, specifically the sons of Ívaldi. About Gungnir it is said "that the spear never

---

[14] Edred, *ALU*, 203.
[15] Bjarni Einarsson, *Egils Saga*, 153.

stopped in its thrust" (*at geirrinn nam aldri staðar í lagi*).[16] In *Ynglinga saga*, a spear point is used to mark a dying man in order to dedicate him to Óðinn.[17] In *Völuspá* 24, Óðinn throws a spear over the Vanir.[18] This ritually starts the war, brings good luck in battle, and dedicates them to him. In *Gautreks saga*, when Starkaðr sacrifices King Víkarr, he says "Now I give you to Óðinn," and the slender reed that he is holding transforms into an actual spear, and Víkarr is stabbed.[19] Óðinn's spear outmatches any earthly weapon. In chapter 11 of *Völsunga saga*, it is said:

> Ok er orrosta hafði staðit um hríð, þá kom maðr í bardagann með síðan hött ok heklu blá. Hann hafði eitt auga ok geir í hendi. Þessi maðr kom á mót Sigmundi konungi ok brá upp geirinum fyrir hann. Ok er Sigmundr konungr hjó fast, kom sverðit í geirinn ok brast í sundr í tvá hluti. Síðan sneri mannfallinu, ok váru Sigmundi konungi horfin heill, ok fell mjök liðit fyrir honum.
>
> The battle had been going on for some time, when a man came into the fight. He had a wide-brimmed hat that sloped over his face, and he wore a black hooded cloak. He had one eye, and he held a spear in his hand. This man came up against King Sigmund, raising the spear before him. When Sigmund struck hard with his sword, it broke in two against the spear. Then the tide of the battle turned, for King Sigmund's luck was now gone, and many of his men fell.[20]

This shows the spear's power to change wyrd—King Sigmund was doing well in the battle, and though he had the smaller force, he might have won. But after his sword is broken by Gungnir, he and his army have no chance, and they are defeated. But spears were not merely for use in battle; they were also ritual objects, as demonstrated by the finds of decorated spearheads (which were clearly not intended for actual use in battle) carved with early

---

[16] Snorri, *Edda*, trans. Faulkes, 97; Snorri, *Edda: Skáldskaparmál*, 1:42.

[17] Snorri, *Heimskringla*, ed. Bjarni, 1:22–23; Snorri, *Heimskringla*, trans. Finlay and Faulkes, 1:13.

[18] *Eddukvæði*, 1:297.

[19] *Seven Viking Romances*, 157.

[20] *Fornaldarsögur Norðurlanda*, 1:26; Byock, *Saga of the Volsungs*, 53

runic inscriptions. One of them, the Spearhead of Dahmsdorf-Müncheberg, is decorated with silver inlay and bears the runic inscription **ranja** (*rannja*, "the runner").[21] *Sigrdrífumál* 18 notes that runes are carved on the point of Gungnir.[22]

A number of different meditation themes may be found in this symbol complex. Runically, it should be noted that the Old English *Gār* rune looks like a combination of *Gebō* and *Ingwaz*. These, interestingly enough, are the first two consonants of Gungnir (g and ng). Pictorially, we might think of this as a god on the gallows. The gar is also the beginning and end of the runes, since Óðinn gained the runes when first pierced by gar, and *Gār* is the final rune of the Anglo-Saxon Futhorc. Ash was a commonly used wood for making spears in ancient times, and the word is used as a *heiti* for a spear. The World Tree is also thought of as an ash, and the first man was said to be made from an ash tree. One can then draw an identification across all three: Ash as man, gar, and tree. The name Gungnir means "the swaying one."[23] It seems to be related to an obscure Danish verb (*gungre*) that means "to tremble." All of this could indicate that the spear had the power to strike fear into people, or perhaps to bring them under Óðinn's influence. It could also be that "the swaying one" is literally Óðinn himself when he was hanging on the tree, and thus the power of his runic initiation has become materialized as the scepter of sovereign authority he wields. The Initiate seeking to expand his knowledge of gar should meditate on all of the above themes.

One may also offer blessings to Óðinn for gar knowledge, since he is the Lord of the Gar. In such blessings, he should be called on with many of his names referring to the spear. These include Geirs Dróttinn (lord of the spear), Geirlöðnir (the one who invites (to battle) with a spear), Geirölnir (the one who rushes forth with a spear), Geirtýr (spear god), Geirvaldr (spear master), Dörruðr (spear fighter), and Sviðrir (spear god).[24] In such blessings, one can use a spear to dedicate an offering (one that is

---

[21] Edred, *Runelore*, 15.
[22] *Eddukvæði*, 2:316–17.
[23] Simek, *Dictionary of Northern Mythology*, 124.
[24] *Skaldic Project*, Heiti, "Óðinn."

preferably being destroyed by fire, but burial or submersion if that is impractical) to Óðinn.

For esoteric use in today's world, I drew upon various gar lore and the Grail Mythos in crafting a short poetic strophe for *Gār* in order to incorporate it into the Old English Rune Poem:

> Gār byþ gum-dōm,   gūðwuda drȳ-wiga:
> wyrde hē wealdeð,   wæl hē cēoseð,
> blōd hē bēoded;   þes brand Wōdnes,
> ungemetum ēacen,   byþ æðele grāl.
>
> Gar is sovereignty, a sorcerer of war-woods:
> it changes the wyrd, it chooses the slain,
> it summons the blood; this brand of Woden,
> enormously mighty, is a noble grail.[25]

This strophe provides a powerful focus for channeling the energies in this symbol, but bear in mind that it also strongly connects it to the Grail Mythos. If you wish to work with gar apart from that mythos, you may want to avoid using this strophe.

With all of this, there are a number of ways that one might incorporate the use of spear symbolism in one's ritual and Rune-Work. For instance, as one begins a daily session of Rune-Work with a recitation of *Hávamál* 138–39, the Runer can try lightly tapping himself with a spear point at the appropriate time in the recitation. In this, the Runer gives himself to himself in emulation of Óðinn, rather than giving himself to Óðinn. One could create and use a rune galdor out of the word **gaizaz* as a way of ritually "wounding" oneself for the metaphorical hanging on the Tree of one's daily Rune-Work. **Gēbō* and **galgōn*, as other names for the rune in Edred's triadic system, can also be worked into such galdors. Although the *Nine Doors of Midgard* does not include a *staða* or *höndstaða* for the *Gār* rune, the enterprising Runer could develop one and add it into a ritual wounding.

---

[25] Westcoat, "Runes for the Grails," 272 (text), 182 (poetic translation). See also in that source the following: for the literal translation, 273; for my background discussion of the spear, 256–58; for esoteric analysis of my *Gār* strophe, 282–85. One should see also the short summary of *gār* lore in Edred, *ALU*, 140–43, which includes some of the material I used in my own synthesis for the rune.

In shape, the spear is similar to the gand in being long and thin. One might then use a spear as a kind of super-gand for elaborate signing and sending workings where a change in wyrd is most essential and yet most difficult to manage by lesser means. At the higher levels of development, one might even be able to lay down wyrd directly into the well through speaking words of power while brandishing a spear as a sign of sovereignty and mastery. A miniature spear-gand might be made for such purposes, or one could craft a full-size spear. Unless one is a blacksmith, it would be necessary to purchase a spearhead and tail cap from those who can make such things. Nevertheless, with the right tools, one can carve powerful runes into that metal spearhead, just as the ancients did. The spear shaft, on the other hand, will be long and wooden, providing a lot of space for the Runer to carve a lengthy inscription empowering the spear. My *Gār* rune strophe above would make a powerful inscription for enchanting such a spear, and since it is in Old English, it would be easy to render it into the correct runes for carving. Advanced Runers might try their hand at their own composition for a *Gār* rune strophe to inscribe. To accompany a carved strophe on the shaft, one might carve a single large *Gār* rune on the spearhead. In this way, one can materialize the essence of the *Gār* rune's power most directly.

Conclusion

For the Runer in Midgard, the road to the Runes is a long one, but it is not alone or empty-handed. The Eagle is within and always watching as you hang on the tree through your Rune-Work. As Óðinn was wounded by gar, you too must be wounded by gar in your own way. Use the knowledge of gar so that you can more effectively emulate Óðinn and pierce yourself with its esoteric power as you are on the Tree. And be aware of the Eagle's presence as the first step toward more effectively feeding your lower self completely to your higher self, so that you will be reborn roaring as your Eagle when you truly take up the Runes. And when you fall back after, you can then take up your Gar again and truly know that you are wielding the power of the Runes with it.

Works Cited

Barnes, Michael P. *Runes: A Handbook*. Woodbridge: Boydell Press, 2012.

Bjarni Einarsson, ed. *Egils saga*. London: Viking Society for Northern Research, 2003.

Byock, Jesse L., trans. *The Saga of the Volsungs: The Norse Epic of Sigurd the Dragon Slayer*. Berkeley: University of California Press, 1990.

Eddukvæði. Edited by Jónas Kristjánsson and Vésteinn Ólason. 2 vols. Reykjavík: Hið íslenzka fornritafélag, 2014.

Edred Thorsson. *ALU: An Advanced Guide to Operative Runology*. San Francisco: Weiser, 2012.

Edred Thorsson. *The Nine Doors of Midgard: A Curriculum of Rune-work*. 5th ed. Moss Beach, CA: The Rune-Gild, 2016.

Edred Thorsson. *Runelore: A Handbook of Esoteric Runology*. Boston: Weiser, 1987.

Fornaldarsögur Norðurlanda. Edited by Guðni Jónsson and Bjarni Vilhjálmsson. 3 vols. Reykjavík: Forni, 1943–1944.

Larrington, Carolyne, trans. *The Poetic Edda*. 2nd ed. Oxford: Oxford University Press, 2014.

Lindow, John. *Norse Mythology: A Guide to the Gods, Heroes, Rituals, and Beliefs*. Oxford: Oxford University Press, 2001.

Seven Viking Romances. Translated by Hermann Pálsson and Paul Edwards. London: Penguin, 1985.

Simek, Rudolf. *Dictionary of Northern Mythology*. Cambridge: D. S. Brewer, 1993.

Skaldic Project. Website, <skaldic.org>, accessed May 25, 2025.

Snorri Sturluson. *Edda*. Translated by Anthony Faulkes. London: Dent, 1987.

Snorri Sturluson. *Edda: Prologue and Gylfaginning*. Edited by Anthony Faulkes. 2nd ed. London: Viking Society for Northern Research, 2005.

Snorri Sturluson. *Heimskringla*. Edited by Bjarni Aðalbjarnarson. 3 vols. 4th, 3rd, and 2nd eds., respectively. Íslenzk fornrit 26–28. Reykjavík: Hið íslenzka fornritafélag, 2002, 2002, and 1979.

Snorri Sturluson. *Heimskringla*. Translated by Alison Finlay and Anthony Faulkes. 3 vols. London: Viking Society for Northern Research, 2011–2015.

Snorri Sturluson. *Edda: Skáldskaparmál*. Edited by Anthony Faulkes. 2 vols. 1998. Corrected reprint, London: Viking Society for Northern Research, 2007.

Tacitus. *The Agricola and the Germania*. Translated by H. Mattingly and revised by S. A. Handford. Baltimore: Penguin Books, 1970.

Tolkien, Christopher, ed. and trans. *The Saga of King Heidrek the Wise*. London: Thomas Nelson, 1960.

Westcoat, Eirik. "Runes for the Grails: Creating Old English Rune Poem Stanzas for Cweorð, Calc, Stān, and Gār." In *Eagle's Mead*, 249–89, 178–82 (poem translation). Long Branch, PA: Skaldic Eagle Press, 2019.

The Canon of Nine: A Spiritual Call to Arms

Introduction
In the early days of this millennium, the Guild of the Grail briefly blazed forth into existence to illuminate a path of Traditional initiatory attainment. In the Guild's literature, it adopted a series of regal precepts called "The Canon of Nine," written by Sir Faustus. However, the Guild's literature had no discussion of those precepts—they were simply stated, without guidance or commentary. Over twenty years later, the modern world has continued to decay, and these precepts are still valuable and in need of expounding to those who seek a Higher Life and would walk the path of Knighthood in that once-and-future Guild. For those seekers, I discuss each of those precepts here. And they are my own interpretations; I don't know if Sir Faustus would agree with them. If one reads the Guild of the Grail's guidebook, *Liber Ars Collegium*, one will undoubtedly find more inspiration there for interpreting and applying these precepts. Nevertheless, this essay is meant to be of benefit even to those who have not read it.

How to Approach the Precepts
Before delving into the precepts, some contextualization is in order. Like the writings of Nietzsche or Evola, they are prone to misunderstanding when approached by a know-it-all who is secretly (or not so secretly) looking to confirm his own prejudices instead of starting on the difficult path of Ascent. And having confronted neither the difficulty of the path nor affirming a genuine desire for Ascent, such a know-it-all will only find his lower self reflected back at him, as his ego deflects the call to self-examination inherent in the precepts.

The first thing to be considered is that these are *regal* precepts, with everything that word entails. In the *New Oxford American Dictionary*, the word *regal* is defined as "of, resembling, or fit for a monarch, especially in being magnificent or dignified." And there can be no doubt that Sir Faustus was thinking of these precepts in just such a manner. The Guild of the Grail expounded an initiatory path of Knighthood, and the virtues of the ideal Knight are entirely appropriate for a King as well. Indeed, one sees that as the ideal in the chivalric literature. There is another reason *regal* is appropriate here as well. These precepts, first and foremost, are about self-governance, an ideal for the individual to follow in ruling himself for his initiatory development. One must rule oneself just as the ideal king rules his country, and in self-rulership, the model of monarchy is the only workable model. (Just try and see if you can envision running your inner self-development as a democracy!)

And how does the wise king govern? Here, I turn to Evola's ideal of the Emperor, expounded most directly in his book, *Heathen Imperialism*. For him, the true Emperor—a fully-functioning channel for the presence of Spirit in the world—rules by a certain spiritual chrism and a majesty within, not by crude violence. That is, the magnificence of his being inspires obedience in his subjects.[1] Also, in the occasions that he has to employ violence, it is done in a detached, impersonal manner—never out of petty vengeance nor a desire to inflict suffering. This kind of view undoubtedly has its roots in Indo-European wisdom, for which the Hindu form can be found in the *Bhagavad-Gītā*:

> Therefore, always perform unattached the deed to be done, for the man (*purusha*) performing action [while being] unattached attains the Supreme.
>
> By action indeed [King] Janaka and others attained [spiritual] consummation. Even considering only the world's welfare, you ought to act.[2]

He seeks justice and right order for the sake of maintaining the society's orientation toward Spirit. Ultimately, it is rulership by a graceful, guiding, and light hand. A Chinese proverb says, "Govern a great nation as you would cook a small fish—don't overdo it." And Henry David Thoreau: "That government is best which governs least." Keep those thoughts in mind while I take a brief detour to discuss the dichotomy of the superior vs. the inferior, which is central to the Canon of Nine.

---

[1] Evola, *Heathen Imperialism*, 47–57, especially 49, 52, and 56.

[2] Feuerstein, *The Bhagavad-Gītā*, 125, verses 3.19–20.

The Canon of Nine

While the Guild of the Grail asserts the primacy of Spirit over matter, this should not be taken as a denigration of matter. The Guild is not a Gnostic organization, even though it appreciates the value of some Gnostic perspectives—matter is not inherently evil for the Guild of the Grail. The material world is Necessary and Good (or perhaps can be made Good)—to assert otherwise would be to reject the West's noble Indo-European religious inheritance. But one must nonetheless choose which principle to place a higher value on, and so the Guild chooses Spirit—one cannot truly be on the Grail Quest otherwise. It is much the same with the Guild's upholding of the majestic over the mundane. In like fashion, the various items of the Canon of Nine should not be construed, in most cases, to absolutely denigrate what is positioned as inferior. Many of the "inferior" items are things that unavoidably exist in the world. Each proposition of the Canon of Nine is a choice between the two ends of a duality. We must choose what to value while remembering that the duality cannot be eliminated while we have a body on the material plane. In regards to such choices, the following tale, called "Two Wolves: A Cherokee Legend," should be kept in mind:

> An old Cherokee is teaching his grandson about life. "A fight is going on inside me," he said to the boy.
>
> "It is a terrible fight and it is between two wolves. One is evil—he is anger, envy, sorrow, regret, greed, arrogance, self-pity, guilt, resentment, inferiority, lies, false pride, superiority, and ego." He continued, "The other is good—he is joy, peace, love, hope, serenity, humility, kindness, benevolence, empathy, generosity, truth, compassion, and faith. The same fight is going on inside you—and inside every other person, too."
>
> The grandson thought about it for a minute and then asked his grandfather, "Which wolf will win?"
>
> The old Cherokee simply replied, "The one you feed."[3]

---

[3] This particular text came from a no-longer-extant website for the First People of America and Canada, Turtle Island. Numerous variants are available online.

And so it is with the two sides of each precept in the Canon of Nine—feed the higher one, the one that is of the Wolf of Spirit within you, give it your love and attention. Do not focus hate, repression, or suppression on the Wolf of matter, because that, in fact, will feed it nonetheless. And so we come back to Evola. Though his ideal for the Outer Imperium as expressed in *Heathen Imperialism* appears impossible to achieve, that is not where its power lies for us in today's world. "As above, so below"—thus, turn those ideals for the Imperium inwards and use them as a model for your own self-transformation, so that you may become the Spirit-centered Emperor over your Inner Imperium. Absolute attainment of this during your life may still be impossible, but you most definitely can make enough progress to bring yourself enormous real benefits—the real benefits that come from aligning yourself with the aspirations of each precept through majesty and wisdom, not the crude violence of repression. One could also bring Jungian psychology ideas into this analysis, particular notions about how things that are repressed into the unconscious will manifest in unhealthy manners, including through projections onto the world and people around oneself. This corresponds to the Emperor who rules through violence rather than majesty, and these repression dynamics have their manifestations just the same, whether it is within the individual or within a society. The reader is invited to contemplate the matter from that angle as well if he finds it beneficial. Now it is time to consider each of the precepts.

1. "Adherence to antiquity is superior to acceptance of modernity"

This precept begins the Canon of Nine by expressing a Traditional outlook toward today's world. Such Traditional ideals, for the most part, were more actualized in ancient cultures. The modern world has a pernicious myth that guides it, the Myth of Progress: the idea that everything is improving and getting better, and that this is a one-way trajectory upwards. A world of endless novelty, where everything new is prized, and the old things are discarded, whether goods or knowledge. The myth, however, is not true, and this precept is a call to reject that myth and see what has been lost. It is a call to seek out antiquity and what is best and noble in it, to

The Canon of Nine

know it and understand it. Then one must prize it, promote it, work for it, fight for it, and live it—that is how one adheres to antiquity while avoiding an acceptance of modernity. One must detach from modernity—fighting against the leviathan would be a fool's errand for virtually anyone, and one must watch out, lest one's hate strengthen it.

Also, rejecting modernity is not about technology, but primarily values, and is thus not a call to discard all of our technology. Modern sanitation and medicine have eliminated most of the disease risks that literally plagued the ancient world. But we could certainly take a more skeptical attitude toward much of the latest gadgetry—ask yourself what you really need, and how it is going to improve your life. Are you really happier because of it? Does it further your goals? Or does it use you to further someone else's goals? The modern world has left many of us alienated from ourselves and each other, without a sense of meaning, and bereft of connection to the transcendent—these things, more than anything else, are what we need to counteract by embracing antiquity.

How best to detach from modernity and adhere to antiquity? The media you consume is as important for your mind as the food you consume is for your body. So consume that which is of antiquity, or which is guided by the best and highest principles that antiquity adhered to. And what might that mean? An excellent place to start would be the five transcendentals identified in the ancient Western philosophical tradition: Truth, Beauty, Justice/Goodness, Love, and Home/Being. This part of the tradition has been affirmed in Western philosophy ever since, through the High Middle Ages and is still active today, including in the recent works of Fr. Robert Spitzer.[4] Ask yourself how the media you are consuming reflect the existence of or the striving toward those five transcendentals, and keep adjusting your "diet" toward these transcendentals. With such antiquity-minded consumption, the wolf of antiquity inside will grow stronger. Look to classic books, art, and movies that reflect these transcendentals and the world of antiquity. But then, more directly, actually seek out knowledge of antiquity itself. Study past centuries and the

---

[4] Spitzer, *Finding True Happiness*, chapter 2.2.

events and literature in them, especially according to your aesthetic and religious sensibilities. If you are a Catholic Christian, learn about life in the Middle Ages, read notable philosophers such as Thomas Aquinas, and appreciate the art and architecture of that period. If you are a Norse Heathen, read the Eddas and Icelandic Sagas and learn about life in the Viking Age. And probably everyone should learn more about ancient Greece and Rome, for if you are a Westerner alive today, they are a foundational influence on our culture that cannot be escaped. It is by drinking from the deep wells of antiquity that we can find new strength to revolt against the modern world.

2. "Self-overcoming is superior to self-acceptance"

Most important for implementing this precept is that which was inscribed in the Temple of Apollo at Delphi: γνῶθι σεαυτόν (*gnōthi seauton*)—"Know thyself!" A certain amount of self-acceptance, in the sense of accurately assessing your current situation and limitations, is necessary for a self-overcoming plan of action. Self-overcoming is a journey, and you cannot plan the journey ahead if you don't know and accept your starting position!

I once dated a woman confined to a wheelchair due to cerebral palsy. Only one of her hands has completely normal functioning. Yet with her motorized wheelchair, she manages a surprising amount of independence nonetheless. She lives alone, without any personal caregiver. Hers is a stellar combination of self-acceptance—she is never going to be free of that wheelchair, and she knows it—and a tremendous drive of self-overcoming in the desire to live as normal of a life as possible. But she would never have managed this if she had lapsed into self-denial about her condition.

You, too, will have to be accurate in assessing your situation, and accept where you are right now, and determine what elements of your situation can be changed at this time and which cannot. Put your work of self-overcoming into those things that can be changed. Quite often, they are more than you might suspect. And take the small steps today that you can if the larger ones are not yet possible—the Great Work is not accomplished in a single day. Start with what you can do now. Perhaps it is cutting out excessive sugar consumption or social media browsing. Or beginning a regular exercise plan. Or putting aside thirty minutes each day to write that novel you've always wanted to write. Actually taking one step today is better than merely thinking about taking ten steps. And keep at it. In time, you will look back on your self-assessment, realize that you've grown, and see new possibilities for self-overcoming: things that previously seemed unchangeable are no longer so.

It is the wisdom of the Emperor that is needed to guide this journey. Your brain and body are malleable and can make great gains with patience and training. They are not instantly changeable, so beware of the violence of short cuts such as overworking with under-sleeping and under-exercising. There may be times when using such short cuts sparingly is necessary, but when you use them all the time, you have fallen into the same trap as the Emperor who is constantly ruling by brute violence. Ultimately, self-overcoming is an endless journey, and at the highest levels, one must embrace this endlessness. If that sounds too intimidating at the moment, return to the advice above about small steps. What is important is that you are on the right path—there are days when you need to be aware of the destination, and other days when it is better to focus on what is right ahead of you and leave tomorrow's cares to tomorrow.

What we ultimately see here is that rather than being *inferior* to self-overcoming in an absolute sense, it is instead the case that self-acceptance is *anterior* to self-overcoming. Self-acceptance is the starting gate, not the finish line, and when we truly realize that, we can prepare for and set out upon our great journey of self-overcoming. It is when we make the mistake of seeing self-acceptance as the end goal that it becomes genuinely inferior to self-overcoming. Through self-acceptance, you have entered the stadium—are you there to watch, or to run the race?

3. "Seeking the unattainable is superior to surrendering to the commonplace"

This is a call to have goals for oneself that are worthy of the regal dignity that a Knight strives for. Perhaps you are one of those people who can be motivated by merely material concerns such as money and the various things that money can buy, and who can be content or even happy with those things as markers of success. But I doubt it, as such people are not likely to be reading this essay. My readers are more likely to be those who are unsatisfied with the modern world, people who feel a yearning for something higher, something better, than the commonplace mundanity around them.

What is the "commonplace" in this precept? It is all around us, all the time, and never far away. And it has always been like this, even in staunchly traditional societies. But it will vary somewhat for everyone, so you must look around in your life and circumstances. For the one who grows up in city slums, surrounded by poverty and crime, the commonplace will be very different from that of one who grows up on a rural farm, milking cows and feeding animals every day. Each of these individuals will have little cause to be concerned with what is commonplace for the other. And while the former might seek to wholly escape from his situation, the latter might not—rather than escape, he might choose to embrace the situation and seek to raise it to its highest potential. And it is okay that many in the world are content with the commonplace. If they are to rise above it, perhaps their time will come eventually, and they will find their own way. But that's okay. These are, after all, *regal* precepts, not *yeomanly* precepts.

If you have decided to rise above the commonplace, how might this be done? "Surrendering to the commonplace" is, in a way, also a sort of outward version of the self-acceptance of the second precept. Similarly, we must acknowledge the commonplace for the same reason, that of knowing our starting position so that we can more effectively plan our Quest. One must be careful with this precept, and remember that despite the positioning here, there is much that is attainable that is most definitely *not* commonplace. We must orient ourselves towards the highest attainable we can manage, one which will bring us ever closer to the unattainable, even though, by definition, it can never be reached. And in this striving, we will take ourselves out of the realm of the commonplace.

Eventually, you will realize that seeking the unattainable is the best way to reach that which is attainable. Those who are in the

Rune-Gild know this, for they seek Rûna, the ultimate Mystery, even while knowing it can never be truly and completely obtained. It is much the same for the true Knight who seeks the Grail. When we are truly guided by such a "distant star in sight" that can never actually be reached, we will not lack for practical goals and way-stations on our endless quest, ones which will bring many tangible benefits.

What unattainable should you seek? If goals such as Rûna and the Grail do not speak to your soul, it is here that one can use the five transcendentals mentioned above—Truth, Beauty, Justice/Goodness, Love, and Home/Being—as a guidepost, for in their absolute forms, they are unattainable also. Contemplate them, and perhaps you will find your distant star in sight thereby. And this is where the great art and architecture of the past had a role. The great cathedrals of the Middle Ages invariably lifted people's minds to the higher realms, to take them away from the commonplace and inspire them with a vision of greatness, so that when they inevitably must return to life among the commonplace, they will have an ideal within to guide them. This is yet another reason why the media you consume is so critical: you need material that will inspire you.

4. "Struggle and strife are superior to comfort and passivity"

I am not one to denigrate comfort in moderation. And even if one wanted to avoid comfort completely in the modern world, it might prove to be more hassle than it is worth. One could go the purely ascetic route, off living in a monastery, forest, or cave. That will have little comfort, but it is also a setting that will avoid much struggle and strife. Evola contrasted the warrior (action) path to the ascetic (contemplation) path,[5] and while both are valid, I am more concerned with the warrior path here, as these are regal precepts, not ascetic precepts, although there is inevitably some overlap, as both partake of the higher realms.

But comfort and passivity are certainly a problem in excess, for exactly the reason that such excess leads to inertia in our lives: a lack of change and a lack of accomplishment. Yet this is perhaps

---

[5] Evola, *Revolt Against the Modern World*, 111–15.

one of the easiest binaries of the precepts to get on the correct side of. By seeking struggle, we will inevitably limit comfort and passivity, and there will be no need to denigrate them or even to actively seek to limit them. We should seek struggle because that is how fortune is won in this world—it is seldom handed to us. To be sure, the "struggle" can vary quite widely. It may be simple and with oneself, in the gym where one is straining to complete one more rep of a deadlift to reach a new personal record. It may be against others, such as when we revise and keep revising a grant application to improve its chances against the dozens or hundreds of others who are chasing the same funding. (We might even "struggle" with the notion of whether we should even be in that particular struggle!) In short, it is in struggling for Ascent that we gain and grow and manifest better and better words and works.

As for strife, the precept does not mean that strife should be sought for its own sake, of course. Strife is negative most of the time. Rather, some amount of strife is the inevitable result of action in the world and seeking our noble goals. If we win the competitive job position or publish a book, we will inevitably receive the ire of competitors and detractors. Most of the time, it comes from their envy, and it amounts to insignificant whining on their part. To be sure, there are times when our envious adversaries can indeed cause us actual trouble. On my own path, I have gained some detractors, and the following quote from William S. Burroughs is never far from my mind. It is popular on the internet, and in most places you will see it without the first and last sentences, but here is the fuller version:

> I am not one of those weak-spirited, sappy Americans who want to be liked by all the people around them. I don't care if people hate my guts, I assume most of them do. The important question is what are they are in a position to do about it. My affections being concentrated on a few people, are not spread all over Hell in a vile attempt to placate sulky, worthless shits.[6]

---

[6] Burroughs, "Early Routines," 14. The piece indicates that it is a collection of pre-publication excerpts from the William S. Burroughs book of the same name. The wording varies slightly in much of its internet transmission.

Rather than be distressed at the strife, we must know when it is necessary and inevitable, so that we can wear it as a badge of honor when appropriate, or counteract our adversaries when they are in a position to do something about their hate for us. That is, we must be aligned with higher goals of Ascent that motivate us to endure necessary strife. Otherwise, unmoored from a sense of purpose, we could fall into the trap of minimizing all strife, both necessary and unnecessary, and that leads to the trap of comfort and passivity.

Should we ever seek to consciously cause strife? Generally not. Usually, that's dishonorable behavior and can drive off friends and allies. There could perhaps be situations in which we need to strike first against enemies, but it takes wisdom to know this. The Knight, although ready for war, must also love peace. Whether we seek to cause it or not, ultimately strife is only to be endured for the sake of higher things and chosen goals. It is never an end goal in itself.

5. "Imitation of the great is superior to paltry innovation"

This hearkens back to the first precept quite directly, for we can easily find great things to imitate by looking to adhere to antiquity. And the flip side of that is equally obvious, that modernity has a lot of paltry innovation to it. Nevertheless, this precept is ultimately atemporal—we can find both great things to imitate and paltry innovation to avoid in any time period. Of course, the paltry is in greater abundance today. The modern world has its pernicious Myth of Progress, which prizes innovation for its own sake. And much of modern art and architecture has fallen into a compounded trap in this regard, in that it will try to surpass the great masters of the past by refusing to acknowledge them, instead innovating wholly independent of them. One does not have to look hard to see the terrible fruits of this approach. And while this precept is not meant to denigrate worthwhile innovation, it is surely meant to denigrate the degenerate kind of innovation for nothing more than its own sake that Progress encourages.

When it comes to imitating the great, the fine arts are one of the most direct examples of this. For instance, Grand Central Atelier is an art movement and school that directly embraces tradition, where the students indeed start by imitating the great artists of the past, learning their techniques, and practicing with the same traditional subjects as the past masters. It is an excellent way to pursue the five transcendentals, for that is what made the past masters what they were: their encounter with and expression of the transcendentals.

Other fields of endeavor have their own past masters to look to. If you are a poet writing in English, look to Shakespeare, Milton, Eliot, or Whitman for recent masters. Consider also foreign masters for the wisdom they offer. And if you are more of a renegade like myself, consider looking to even older poetry: *Beowulf*, the Old Norse skalds, and so forth. If you are an academic, look to the scholars whose scholarship has stood the test of time, and you will find models of clarity and brilliance to follow. And if you are an academic, I certainly don't need to point out how the field today is rife with novelty for the mere sake of novelty—its equivalent of paltry innovation—let alone the numerous other problems of the field.

Fields not usually thought of as creative have their own past masters to imitate as well. In politics, read biographies of people like Teddy Roosevelt, Thomas Jefferson, or George Washington. If you are a pilot, consider the examples of great aviators of the twentieth century. Whatever field you are in, it has its past masters, and you can learn from the excellence of their craft and their personal habits for cultivating success. Ironically enough, it is through imitation of the great that innovation will creep into your work, but instead of being paltry or contrived, it will be genuine and useful. That's how proper innovation actually works, and one of the greatest traditionalists of our times, Roger Scruton, aptly summarized Eliot's views on the matter: "True originality is possible only within a tradition—and further, that every tradition must be remade by the genuine artist, in the very act of creating something new."[7]

As you may have noticed, I have not said all that much about paltry innovation (especially in terms of concrete examples) in this section, and there is a simple reason. Like many of the other precepts, this is one where a strong focus on the superior end of

---

[7] Scruton, "T.S. Eliot as Conservative Mentor."

the binary—imitation of the great—is all that is required. Sufficiently focused on that, you will avoid paltry innovation without having to give it much thought.

6. "Right action is superior to personal convenience"

This is a more clear-cut guideline, as the two principles here are generally independent. That is, whether a particular action is right is typically not a function of its convenience. Of course, we notice such matters only when right action happens to be opposed to personal convenience, which is what this precept is really about—taking right action when it is difficult to do, since virtually everyone takes right action when it is easy to do. That is why a Knight is a truly Knight, because he does the right things, especially when they are difficult to do.

The biggest challenge, here, of course, is determining what "right action" is for yourself. And not just in unusual circumstances. The brave hero who dashes into a burning building to rescue a trapped child has certainly chosen right action over personal convenience. But this is a rarity, as only the tiniest number of us will ever face such a situation. We must instead seek to apply this precept in our everyday lives and in situations that we will encounter quite frequently—that is the only way to get any real value out of this precept. And right action will change over time. What is right action for you today might well be wrong action if you did it again one year from now.

Therefore, you must have a clear idea of your goals and your purpose in this world. Yes, you can uphold Tradition and Quest for the Grail. But how, precisely, will you do that, and in what context? Everyone's Quest is different. Mine is a combination of poet and scholar who pursues Óðrœrir, the legendary Old Norse Mead of Inspiration. Your Quest will be different. You might be creating a new startup business. Or you might have a family and children to support. Or you might be studying to become a nurse or surgeon to treat and save the sick and injured.

It is here that the Hindu concept of *dharma* (duty, law, purpose) is important: "Better is one's own *dharma* imperfectly carried out than another's *dharma* well performed."⁸ That leads us to the first right action one must undertake—the discovery of one's *dharma*. Then, right action consists in fulfilling one's *dharma*. And this is really the best way, for one who knows his *dharma* and embraces it will feel a much stronger sense of motivation toward right action than one who is adrift and purposeless in this modern world. The former will perhaps not even need this precept, whereas the latter will be unable to care for it. Therefore, this precept calls upon those who are in the middle to choose and take the first step on the path to *dharma*.

As for the personal convenience that tempts us away from right action, it can be many things. It can be the mind-numbing lure of television and social media that calls us away from writing, exercise, or spiritual practices. It can be the cowardice that tempts us into silence and submission instead of standing up for our companions when they are unjustly attacked by woke slanderers. It can be the inertia of staying in a familiar, but unsatisfying job when you've dreamed of doing something different for years. The best way to resist such temptations, ultimately, is to stay connected with your *dharma*. It really all does come down to that.

7. "To be strong and alone is superior to being weak and consorted"

To be clear, there is nothing wrong with being consorted on its own. This precept is a rather complex conjunction of matters. Also, by itself, being alone is not a good position to be in, especially in the context implied by this precept. What is really going on here is a way of emphasizing that it is better to be strong than to be weak, and that this is preferable even when the strength is paired with adverse circumstances and the weakness is paired with favorable circumstances.

It hardly needs to be said that weakness is never an asset. Being weak, quite simply, limits our capacity for action in the world and increases our dependence on others. I am not arguing for absolute independence as preferable—independence is

---

⁸ Feuerstein, *The Bhagavad-Gītā*, 313, verse 18.47, modified slightly from the original.

something that must be cultivated in order to properly engage in interdependence, since interdependence is necessary for a whole slew of successful actions in the world, especially the ones that bring the most change to the world. While we are living in society, we can never be completely free of dependence on others, but this needs to be kept to a reasonable minimum commensurate with our dignity.

As for strength, it is not said what kind is meant here, so one should assume it is all kinds of strength: of muscles, mind, character, talent, vision, spirit, and so forth. The precept is a call to seek more strength, in whatever kinds of strength are best for you (see the preceding precept regarding right action and *dharma*). Strength, of whatever kind, increases our capacity for action and pursuing our goals.

But the precept is really a warning that if we seek to strengthen ourselves, our current friends and acquaintances will sense the change in us, and some of them might not like it. Our growth and pursuit of our dreams may remind them of their stasis, consciously or not, and they may resent us for our daring. Of course, you may be lucky and have friends who are inspired to join you in a path of Ascent. But that is the luck of the draw. So you will need to be prepared to lose the friends who resent your growth. What you can console yourself with is that such friends were never truly your friends—it was a relationship of convenience. And to be fair, maybe it was a matter of convenience for you as well, but only you can know what you saw in them. Real friends will celebrate your growth. Beyond friends, society at large may start treating you differently. Today's society has a complicated relationship with strength. It needs the strength of its great men and women, whether soldiers, scientists, statesmen, and so forth, yet it frequently fears that strength. Indeed, it often seems to denigrate strength, despite celebrating it in some ritualistic forms, such as professional sports. Be prepared for your life to change if you seek strength, for you will also accrue detractors, which I have addressed with precept four above.

Continuing in that vein, the way to find proper balance in this precept is by subjecting it to the other precepts, notably the preceding one about right action. We should always try to increase our strength in all ways, and this may make us more alone, and a grounding in right action must guide us in deciding just how much aloneness we should embrace for the sake of strength, whether we should find another way to increase our strength, or whether knowledge of our *dharma* indicates that our strength is exactly where it needs to be and that we should focus our right action elsewhere.

8. "The aristocratic is superior to the egalitarian"

This precept is especially complementary to precepts one and five. Egalitarianism is an aspect of modernity, but it is by no means the whole of modernity. Likewise, the aristocratic is part of antiquity, and not the whole of antiquity either. More than any of the other precepts, this one identifies the Guild of the Grail as an elitist organization—but it is one that looks to a traditional view of what is elite, as opposed to modern plutocratic systems based on wealth.

Prying into the word's origin is the way to go here. It is from a Greek root, ἄριστος (*áristos*), meaning "best," whereas egalitarian goes back to Latin *aequalis*, meaning "equal." And so we are called to seek the best, and choose the best, making this a priority over that which is equal. Following traditional principles, we know that human beings can never truly be equal. They may be granted a political equality of rights and opportunities, but humans vary extraordinarily widely in talent, health, character, and so forth. Even among identical twins (and I know, because I am one), one still finds many differences, despite an identical genetic endowment and what are usually very similar upbringings. Human beings are no more equal than a poodle and a golden retriever are equal, yet the breeds both share a common dignity as dogs, and we all share a common dignity as humans. Yet in the degeneracy of the modern world, people on all ends of the political spectrum are frequently confusing political equality with actual equality and/or with fundamental dignity.

Like several of the prior precepts, this is another one in which adherence to the superior will get the job done, without needing to concern oneself with the avoidance of the inferior. But it is a helpful consideration insofar as where things are equal and egalitarian, things are usually not the best they can be. Whether in material goods, actions, speech, or whatever else, to pursue the best and the aristocratic necessarily means leaving behind the egalitarian. So dress to a better standard, get yourself in shape so that you have a better figure, read better books, and watch better movies. If your monetary means are limited, start with what has the least cost—exercise is always an option, even if it is just doing pushups on your floor or going for a jog around the neighborhood. But there is not just simply one possibility for dressing more aristocratic and so forth—there are many in today's world, and here, *dharma* is your best guide for which way to do it. And again, as always, the five transcendentals make a great guide in pursuing this precept, for the aristocratic necessarily aims itself in that direction, while the egalitarian does not.

We can pursue the aristocratic in many realms. One may, for instance, take the habit of smoking as an illustration of this. If you are caught up in smoking cigarettes—which are rather egalitarian (and also plebeian, see the next precept)—consider switching to cigars, even if it is to the lower end of the cigar spectrum, for cigars are certainly a more aristocratic form of tobacco. And it likely will be a switch—most people I know either smoke one or the other: the sort who smokes both cigarettes and cigars with equal fervor doesn't seem to exist. Ultimately, embracing cigars will force out the cigarettes. And you will likely be smoking less, as cigars are more expensive, and instead starting to enjoy and savor the experience for its finer qualities when you do, rather than simply treat it as a quick fix of nicotine to be administered daily.

For the record, I myself smoke cigars, and I had actually started with cigars. Even being in the presence of friends who smoked cigarettes, I didn't switch to cigarettes, although I did start smoking cigarillos (and I don't inhale these, because I like my lungs), as I was in an environment that seldom provided a good location for enjoying cigars. It also makes the point that my inner sense of direction in this matter was strong enough that rather than take up their habit, I came up with a way to enjoy my own, albeit in a limited manner. This is also to make the point that the choice between the aristocratic and the egalitarian is all around us, all the time—not in a far-off, rarefied realm.

9. "Nobility and restraint are superior to plebeianism and vulgarity"

Here we have a pair of dualities put into juxtaposition, making this a somewhat complex precept. We might wonder why it was not made into separate precepts of nobility/plebeianism and restraint/vulgarity. We might also wonder how it differs from the previous precept, which is easier to say: plebeianism and vulgarity are not at all the same as the egalitarian, although nobility and the aristocratic have a lot more overlap.

Avoiding plebeianism is simple. It is to eschew what pertains to the common people and the vices of the common people. But one must avoid the trap of hating them. The plebes have their place in the world, and many of them may be kind, generous, and good-natured people—the best of them are on their own path of Ascent, and it will unfold for them in their own time and lifetimes. As for vulgarity, the word comes out of *vulgar*, which means "that which is lacking sophistication or good taste; unrefined; characteristic of or belonging to the masses." So it is a combination of that which pertains to the plebeians and that which is the opposite of aristocratic, which have been dealt with here and in the previous precept. Yet here, vulgarity is specifically contrasted to restraint.

Nobility means cultivating a more refined manner and bearing. One must demonstrate a different quality of being than the plebeian, and that means avoiding the vulgarities of the plebeians, and instead practicing the restraint and refinement of the aristocratic, for restraint goes hand in hand with a noble bearing. It is, after all, the plebeians that are associated with crude appetites and indulgences. I don't begrudge them that—the labors they often perform in life are harsh, and only a monster would begrudge them the simple things that give them joy and respite in a frequently unpleasant existence.

But what is this all really about? Ultimately, if these precepts resonate with you, they are a call to embrace a higher life, and this last precept is the most direct about it. You must realize for yourself whether your spirit is with the nobility or the plebeians. If it is with the plebeians, then I wish you well on your own path, although it is not the one that I am offering guidance for here. But if your spirit is with the nobility, this is a call to embrace that reality. And so if you are called to the nobility, you must embrace restraint as one of the most important items in your toolbox. I'm sure I don't need to dwell on the phrase "delayed gratification." It is appropriate to enjoy pleasures in life when it is done in moderation. And moderation is the guiding hand of restraint, since restraint as a virtue is found in the middle between the extremes of too much and too little.

Simply put, if you are called to the nobility, you must hold yourself to a higher standard than the plebeians. In former times, it was the nobility that ruled over the populace. And no one is fit to rule others if they cannot first rule themselves, and so one called to the nobility must first rule over himself. That's still a good and necessary thing for the true nobles of today, even if they are not ruling over others anymore. (In our Western democracies, we are increasingly being ruled over by people who are less and less noble.) For most people, self-rulership is something they can only handle in very limited amounts. Those who are truly plebeian in their hearts need rule from outside, whether it is in the form of a boss at their job, or a strong conviction in religious faith to guide their morality according to traditional precepts. They can be content, and even thrive, with much of their lives being decided for them, whether by overt rulers or the mere chance of the circumstances that mold them. But the true noble must take charge of his own life, and remake it according to his own inner vision. Once again, this comes down to *dharma* and the call to Ascent.

Wrap Up: A Call to Arms

The Canon of Nine is not for the plebeians or the yeomen. Instead, it is a spiritual call to arms for those who are of a different substance, those who are of the spiritual Knighthood in their hearts. It is a challenge for those Knights to walk a higher path, one that will restore their connection to the transcendent. And for those of you who are inspired to follow these precepts and put to the test whether you are one of those Knights, we might finish with a final precept: forgiveness. But not of other people. Forgiveness of yourself. None of us will be perfect in the application of these precepts, least of all me. When we face the inevitable failure in applying them, we must have compassion for and forgive ourselves, so that we pick ourselves up and try again. The Great Work is a long process.

If you are indeed inspired to answer this call to arms, know this: it is a lack of connection to Spirit that is the root of much ill in today's world. And though much of our world has abandoned Spirit, Spirit has not abandoned us. Though the world has driven out Spirit, Spirit will irrupt back into it, always seeking a return. The Guild of the Grail was perhaps one such irruption. There are many such irruptions going on all over the place today, and they will continue. The Canon of Nine is a call to participate in this process. And if you walk a higher path, perhaps Spirit will irrupt into you as well, as you become ever more the spiritual Emperor of your inner Imperium.

Works Cited

Burroughs, William S. "Early Routines." In *Re/Search #4/5: A Special Book Issue*, edited by Vale, 12–15. San Francisco: Re/Search, 1982.

Evola, Julius. *Heathen Imperialism*. Translated by Rowan Berkeley. Edited by Cologero Salvo and Hadi Fakhoury. Thompkins & Cariou, 2007.

Evola, Julius. *Revolt Against the Modern World*. Translated by Guido Stucco. Rochester, VT: Inner Traditions, 1995.

Faustus, Sir. *Liber Ars Collegium*. The Guild of the Grail, 2001.

Feuerstein, Georg, with Brenda Feuerstein, trans. *The Bhagavad-Gītā: A New Translation*. Boston: Shambhala, 2011.

Grand Central Atelier. <grandcentralatelier.org>.

Scruton, Roger. "T.S. Eliot as Conservative Mentor." Available variously on the internet. The original publication appears to be in *The Intercollegiate Review* 39, no. 1–2 (Fall 2003 / Spring 2004): 44–54.

Spitzer, Fr. Robert J. *Finding True Happiness: Satisfying Our Restless Hearts*. Vol. 1 of *Happiness, Suffering, and Transcendence*. San Francisco: Ignatius Press, 2015.

Towards a Meta-Order of Tradition: The Once-and-Future Guild of the Grail

Introduction and Rationale

Tradition, in the capital-T sense, is a popular idea these days. It is, however, in many ways, a difficult, abstract, and transcendent concept. How then are we to make the best use of Tradition, actualize it in our lives, and thereby fulfill one of its intended purposes, that of channeling Spirit from the transcendent world in order to make tangible, beneficial changes in the manifest world? There are doubtless many avenues in which this can take place. In this essay, I will talk about one specific such avenue: the creation of an esoteric initiatory order. And I don't mean a new one. Instead, I am referring to an obscure, short-lived order that briefly manifested in the early years of the millennium: the Guild of the Grail, a Meta-Order of Tradition. It lived once, and perhaps it can live again—just like Arthur, the once-and-future king.

Definitions and Concepts

Terms and concepts that are unfamiliar to some of my readers must now be introduced in their proper turn so that it can be understood just what a "Meta-Order of Tradition" is and why the Guild of the Grail is one. Generally, in this essay, I will use "tradition," lowercase-t, to indicate specific traditions, whether historical or revived in modern times. I will use "Tradition," capital-T, to indicate something like the Traditionalist ideas of Evola, Guénon, and others—note also that capital-T Tradition, in this sense, is only used (and only can be) in the singular. If extra clarity or emphasis is desired or necessary, I will say things like "lowercase-t tradition versus capital-T Tradition," but that is obviously a bit cumbersome. I will not go into an extensive definition of Tradition here. I will say that I consider the relation between tradition and Tradition to be a more-or-less exact parallel to the concept of Platonic Ideals. For instance, such as actual dogs relate to the Platonic Ideal of Dog, but the reader should not make too much of that analogy, as traditions do not exist in the manifest world in the same way that dogs exist in the manifest world. By esoteric initiatory orders, I am referring to groups like the Dragon Rouge, the Rune-Gild, the Hermetic Order of the Golden Dawn, the Temple of Set, and the OTO, among others. These are generally characterized by a system of degrees or other regulated curriculum of study in esoteric or occult work. Techniques such as meditation, divination, and magic are typical of these orders.

Traditions in the general sense tend to take on a life of their own, and they can grow and evolve, or decay and devolve. What conditions this process? The human beings who are the carriers of a tradition, since a tradition can only be a living thing if it is manifested and actualized in living human beings. If a tradition is today only recorded in books and exists nowhere else in a living form, then it is a dead tradition. Can a dead (or mostly dead) tradition be revived? Yes, but it is a lot of work. The Rune-Gild revived the runic tradition, for instance. The Israelis revived Hebrew as a living language. Reviving a tradition is always a heroic task, and should be approached with the appropriate seriousness, but that is not the main subject here.

A proper realm—whether at the level of a society, a city, an organization, a family, or an individual human being—can vivify and vitalize itself by a connection to Spirit, to the Transcendent, and use that connection to channel the beneficence of the transcendent world into the manifest world. It is the same for the bearers of a tradition. If they consciously seek to align themselves with the transcendent world, they can keep their tradition vivid and vital. If instead they cut themselves off from anything higher than themselves, decadence will eventually set in. And so, in the parlance of this philosophy, one calls "Tradition" the power in the transcendent world that is sought for vivifying a tradition. In other words, this expresses my belief that an earthly spiritual tradition, properly maintained, is in some sense fed by spiritual Tradition in the transcendent world. Does that mean that I think that Evola (or Guénon or whoever) was correct in every particular about what Tradition actually is? Of course not. As a Platonic Ideal, Tradition cannot actually exist in the manifest world, anymore than the Platonic Ideal of Dog can actually exist in the physical world. This is partly because Platonic Ideals are perfect, and perfect things cannot exist in the manifest world. This is also because Tradition in the transcendent world does not have a form, nor does it have the quality of particularity—traditions in the manifest world always have a form, and are always particular to their circumstances and the human beings who are manifesting them.

Thus, one cannot *directly* have an initiatory order of Tradition in the manifest world for the same reasons—an initiatory order in the manifest world must necessarily have some form and particularity, so manifest orders must necessarily correspond to manifest traditions, for the most part. So the next best thing that can be done is to have an order of multiple traditions and structure it such that the inter- and intra-play in the traditions of that order promotes the initiatory development of the initiates in such a fashion as to prepare them to take the Olympian metaphysical leap from traditions to Tradition in their esoteric understanding. It would be analogous to attempting to ascertain the Platonic Ideal of Dog from a thorough understanding of numerous manifestations of dogs. An order of this type is ultimately what I mean by a Meta-Order of Tradition.

Orders and Traditions

Now some actual orders may be considered to see how they fit into the picture so far. I start with the Rune-Gild, and it is the one that I am most familiar with. Following two years as an associate, I have been an initiated member of it since late 2011, and a Rune-Master since summer 2016. The Rune-Gild is straightforwardly an initiatory order of tradition, specifically the Germanic rune tradition. In working the process of initiation, one uses runes for divination. Divinatory methods from other cultures, such as the Tarot or I-Ching, are in no way under the official purview of the Rune-Gild. Does that mean one can use nothing other than runes? No, anything of traditional Germanic provenance is acceptable, but it would generally be used secondarily to runes. Indeed, a rudimentary form of omen-taking via birds is discussed in *Runecaster's Handbook* for the purpose of seeking corroboration for a runecast.[1] It is similar with magic—the primary methods involve runes, the initiates are instructed in them, and experimenting with

---

[1] Edred, *Runecaster's Handbook*, 86.

outside additions to rune-magic methods (such as adding planetary hours or other kinds of astrological elections) are at the discretion of the individuals once they have sufficiently mastered the basics of runes. And it is by founding design and internal culture that the Rune-Gild takes and continues this runes-first approach to its tradition. Indeed, I would go so far as to say that the Rune-Gild is a first-rate example of a lowercase-t traditional school and revival of a tradition. More pointedly, the Rune-Gild's founder considers the Gild and its aims to be quite compatible with Tradition.[2]

To this, one may contrast the Temple of Set, which I consider an example of a meta-order, a setup which has proven its effectiveness in creating effective initiates and sustaining the Temple through many decades and a number of internal crises. Although the Temple has its particular mythos of Set as the first principle of isolate intelligence and certain common rituals to hold the group together, it generally appears that members are free to pursue their own specific techniques and working styles for self-transformation. For instance, one might use tarot for divination, another the I-Ching—there is no overriding standard that all are mandated to use, for, as Crowley said, "Every man and woman is a star."

What makes the Temple a meta-order is the formal structuring of the central mythology and common rituals vis-à-vis the various magical traditions that the individual initiates can use for their self-development. This is through the Temple's various Orders, each dedicated to particular specialties and aesthetics, yet still under the umbrella of the Temple as a whole. Generally, an Order is headed by a IV° initiate, and each Order only admits initiates who have obtained at least the II° in the Temple. For instance, the Order of the Trapezoid is broadly dedicated to Germanic mysteries, Runes, and the Grail Quest. (In some sense, this Order is like a Temple equivalent of the Rune-Gild, except far more eclectic than the Rune-Gild would allow, but the reader should not make too much of that analogy. And it should also be

---

[2] Edred, *ALU*, 31–33, a section titled "The Concept of *Traditional* Runelore and Rune-Work."

pointed out that while the Order is most notable for a Germanic focus, its actual purview is wider than that.) Other Orders in the Temple deal with other approaches, such as Egyptian or Vampyric work. A Celtic-themed Order that made special use of Ogham and sought to find manifestations of Set in the Celtic mythology would be possible, but does not exist at this time as far as I know—it would be a matter of whether there were initiates inspired to form such an Order. As everyone joins the Temple at only the I°, the I° does not work within an Order, but instead within the Temple's basic curriculum. That is, the initiate is onboarded into the common culture of the Temple and its unifying idioms and practices regarding Set and the Black Flame, and only then may he go on to specialist study in practices and rituals that will be unique to a small group within the Temple, as opposed to the Temple at large.

Why isn't the Temple a Meta-Order of Tradition? Simply because it is not organized around Evola- and Guénon-style Traditionalism at all—it is organized around Set and the Black Flame. Furthermore, the individual Orders do not constitute traditions in the sense of being strict historical manifestations of Tradition, nor do they try to be, and the orders are all rather too eclectic to a greater or lesser degree. This is all well and good for the Temple, and it has had great success on its path. But the Temple appears to have had one initiate, most likely in its Order of the Trapezoid, who seems to have looked at the structure of the Temple as a meta-order and realized the possibilities for applying this structure to Tradition.[3] That initiate was Sir Faustus, who apparently quit the Temple of Set at the time and founded the Guild of the Grail as a wholly separate organization on June 21, 2001. Alas, the Guild of the Grail was short-lived. At some point after June 2002, Sir Faustus left the Guild. Everyone remaining was only of the 1°, and no progress was possible, so the Guild of the Grail ceased accepting new members, became non-initiatic,

---

[3] The original Guild of the Grail's guidebook, *Liber Ars Collegium*, had a number of "tells" in it that strongly point to its creator having come from the Temple of Set and the Order of the Trapezoid. These include the material about Rûna, among other things.

and quietly disbanded at some point after that. I was not a member of the original Guild of the Grail or even aware of its existence at the time, but I would later (roughly around 2006, give or take) find some of the Guild's documents online. I found them to be an inspiring read with an uplifting message, but did little with them at the time. Yet they persistently stayed in the back of my mind. Later, in late 2013, as a result of my own initiatory development, the documents inspired me in a much greater fashion. This led me to eventually track down what I believed to be nearly all of the original Guild's documents, at least all of the ones that Sir Faustus had shared with anyone in the original Guild. The documents mostly amount to the Guild's guidebook, *Liber Ars Collegium*, in both its public and private manifestations. I have worked with this material since then.[4] I find both the Grail Mythos and Traditionalism fascinating, and the material offered a structured way to approach the combination of the two, which was created by someone quite knowledgeable about both. As to further reasons why I worked with it, the reader will need to see my other essays in this book.

The Meta-Order of Tradition

Now we may turn to the Guild of the Grail's approach. It indeed is focused on Tradition, as Traditionalist thinkers such as Evola and Guénon feature extremely prominently in the Guild's reading lists, especially in the level one books, which are considered essential for a proper understanding of the Guild. In level one from Evola, there is *The Mystery of the Grail, Revolt Against the Modern World, Introduction to Magic*, and *The Hermetic Tradition*. From Guénon there is *The Reign of Quantity and the Signs of the Times* and *The Crisis of the Modern World*. There's much more to level one, which had forty-six books in the original reading list, but Evola and Guénon are a notable chunk that exceeds ten percent. Furthermore, the first three of those Evola books were reckoned

---

[4] The reader may be able to find the old, public version of *Liber Ars Collegium* still lurking somewhere on the internet. There is much that is great in it, as well as things I disagree with, but this essay is not the place to enter into a thorough critique of *Liber Ars Collegium*.

among the five most critical books for the Guild, showing the importance of his Traditionalist thinking for the Guild.

I also consider the Guild of the Grail, as Sir Faustus originally planned it, to be a meta-order. Sir Faustus never uses the term "meta-order," but this quotation from him takes us toward it:

> The G∴G∴ needs many avenues of theurgical Work explored and enacted—for example, I would like to see one Initiate Working with the Runes, another with Renaissance-era "grimoire" magic, another with applied alchemy, and yet another with Crowley's methods. In this way the Guild shall serve as an initiatic "umbrella" under which a variety of practices are being studied.[5]

I second his charge, and I shall expound further on it to explain why having such a variety of practices under one umbrella is both good and necessary for a proper Meta-Order of Tradition. But, in and of itself, what is stated in the quotation does not make the Guild of the Grail a meta-order of Tradition—after all, that quotation more-or-less accurately describes the Temple of Set as well. But first, one more important quotation from Sir Faustus:

> It is nonetheless necessary that we create and introduce a true and legitimate nexus of G∴G∴-specific rites and ceremonial observances into our Work agenda. This does not entail the construction of a magical "system" as such . . . , but rather the recognition and enactment of rites which will serve to embody our principles, illustrate our symbolism, and thus empower our Initiates, our Order, and its egregore.[6]

As indicated, the Guild was not to create a fully elaborated system of esoteric initiation and magic for developing the Self. To be clear on what that means, one example of such a fully elaborated system would include the Rune-Gild's *Nine Doors of Midgard*. Other orders, such as the OTO and the Hermetic Order of the Golden Dawn, have their own systems. Those two quotations are enough to indicate the Guild's disposition as a meta-order, and one of

---

[5] Sir Faustus, *Liber Ars Collegium*, in a section titled "Introduction to G∴G∴ Ritual and Ceremonial Procedures."

[6] Sir Faustus, *Liber Ars Collegium*, again in the section titled "Introduction to G∴G∴ Ritual and Ceremonial Procedures."

broadly analogous structuring compared to the Temple of Set, and it is unsurprising that Sir Faustus would create something similar to his initiatic origins.

As far as "a true and legitimate nexus of G∴G∴-specific rites and ceremonial observances," this revolves around the supremely appropriate center that Sir Faustus chose for the Guild, in the sense that it has elements of a tradition that are most amenable to Tradition itself: the Grail. The Grail Mythos is surely the most rich, interesting, and enduring mythology to come out of post-pagan Europe, bar none. And it has points of contact to numerous traditions throughout Europe, whether Celtic, Christian, Hermetic, or otherwise. Indeed, the Grail itself and the stories about it may be seen as an irruption of Tradition into the world of the Middle Ages. And the supreme story of the Grail, Wolfram von Eschenbach's *Parzival*, embodies the idea of the Grail as a benefic influence from the transcendent world for guiding the manifest world into right order and goodness, and it does this far better than any other Grail romance. I said above that Tradition lacks particularity, and so representing it by a particular tradition has its limitations. Nevertheless, we must work with the traditions we have, and I think it is clear enough that the Grail is the best one we have for such a purpose today, and better than we could have expected or deserved in this decadent modern world.

How then can the Guild of the Grail be a Meta-Order of Tradition? It is to be so by the mutual enrichment of its members through their different traditions. In the course of reaching Knighthood in the Guild of the Grail, the initiate is first heavily steeped in the common core of Traditionalist readings and certain ritual practices particular to the Guild, the work of the 1° to 2° transition. Then the initiate is to work in a traditional system of initiation, or one which has valid remnants of a tradition in the work of the 2° to 3° transition. Each initiate chooses a tradition according to his nature—I am suited to runes; someone else might be more suited to hermeticism. And for many of us, that may mean joining a formal organization such as the Rune-Gild, the OTO, or something else dedicated to a particular tradition, or, at minimum, interacting and learning from those in a particular tradition, even if there is not a formal membership arrangement involved. Once sufficiently ripe, the initiate becomes a 3° Knight in the Guild of the Grail. Interacting among themselves and others, Knights steeped in a diversity of traditions can further their mutual growth and understanding of Tradition in a fuller way than is possible with lone individuals who only have knowledge of a single tradition. In a way, this is analogous to how the academic field of Indo-European Studies makes progress—a scholar in that field must master a number of the descendant languages and cultures, such as Greek, Sanskrit, Roman, Celtic, Persian, etc., which enable a grasp of their common origin. That is, a thorough knowledge of the branches enables an understanding of the trunk and the roots.

The Guild certainly has the potential to create orders within itself that are dedicated to different traditions in order to promote this process. But it must be careful in this regard—the Orders in the Temple of Set are not necessarily traditions vis-à-vis Tradition. So a traditional order in the Guild of the Grail would probably have to resemble the Rune-Gild in some regard, in it being dedicated to something that is a historical tradition or the deliberate revival of a tradition. To recall my earlier Celtic example, one could envision a Guild-internal order devoted solely to the Celtic tradition, which used Ogham and elements of the mythology. This would be possible for other traditions as well, such as alchemy. Alternatively, an order in the Guild could involve new ways to apply traditions to the idea of spiritual Knighthood and the Grail in the service of Tradition—in my own case, if I were to create such an internal order in a revived Guild of the Grail, it would involve the intersection of the Runes and the Grail Mythos. Edred has already written briefly about the combination of the two, and I have applied that material in my own work.[7] But that is distinct from something that is directly a revival of a tradition.

---

[7] Edred, *ALU*, 205–08, an appendix titled "Grail Mythos in Old English Runes?"; Westcoat, "Runes for the Grails."

To What Further End?

Lastly, it is briefly worth considering why a Meta-Order of Tradition is useful and necessary. Let us continue with these words from Sir Faustus:

> In keeping with such a rationale, the Guild of the Grail comes forth at the dawn of a new Millennium to bear witness to just such a timeless and eternally valid Spirit; it is an idea whose time is at hand. Its Chosen Task is to represent an Ideal, to live by a Standard, to reawaken a Royal Path of spiritual attainment amid a world of confusion, ignorance, pseudo-spirituality, and decline masquerading as progress.[8]

And, furthermore, the Guild is about the transformation of individuals, in accordance with Sir Faustus's vision:

> We will—if we are successful as an Order and as Guildsmen—illuminate a path towards the formation of sovereign, aristocratic, and unwavering *individuals*—no more and no less. We will not save "the world" or "humanity" in any broad sense, but we *may* point the way for those rare individuals left today who, as Evola expressed it, ". . . experience a confused and yet real need for liberation, though they do not know in the name of what."[9]

However, one could end up quite lonely as a Man of Tradition in today's world. And that's another critical purpose of the Guild of the Grail as a Meta-Order—mutual support in the seeking of Tradition in a world that does not understand it and is often needlessly hostile to it. Look at any bonfire—even after it has burned down a bit, the coals stay hot if they are together, but if you take one of the coals and move it some distance out of the fire, it will quickly become cold. A proper connection to Tradition can keep us spiritually hot throughout our lives, but it is only the extremely advanced who could do this in isolation in a hostile world—the rest of us need camaraderie and mutual support on the long road to get to such a state, so that we do not become cold.

---

[8] Sir Faustus, *Liber Ars Collegium*.

[9] Sir Faustus, "To Be a Guildsman."

Conclusion

In the Guild of the Grail, all of the necessary elements are in place: It is dedicated to Tradition. In the Grail itself, it has a well-chosen traditional symbol to represent Tradition, one that symbolizes the irruption of Tradition into the manifest world. And it has the structure to bring in initiates in numerous different traditions so that they may work together, whether or not they create their own internal orders dedicated to those traditions. After all, it is only by working in individual traditions that one can gain an appreciation of Tradition—one cannot work directly in a Platonic Ideal—and then in their interactions together, the initiates can learn of other traditions in a way most amenable to attaining Tradition. The great goal of this is the Guild of the Grail's Knighthood, a community of Knights in different traditions who can interact and work together to enhance their understanding of capital-T Tradition in order to use the inspiration of their individual traditions to further the manifestation of Tradition in the world and their continued individual growth. This is what it means to have a Meta-Order of Tradition in the world today.

Works Cited

Edred Thorsson. *ALU: An Advanced Guide to Operative Runology*. San Francisco: Weiser, 2012.

Edred Thorsson. *Runecaster's Handbook: The Well of Wyrd*. York Beach, ME: Weiser, 1999.

Evola, Julius. *The Hermetic Tradition: Symbols and Teachings of the Royal Art*. Translated by E. E. Rehmus. Rochester, VT: Inner Traditions, 1995.

Evola, Julius. *The Mystery of the Grail: Initiation and Magic in the Quest of the Spirit*. Translated by Guido Stucco. Rochester, VT: Inner Traditions, 1996.

Evola, Julius. *Revolt Against the Modern World*. Translated by Guido Stucco. Rochester, VT: Inner Traditions, 1995.

Evola, Julius, and the UR Group. *Introduction to Magic: Rituals and Practical Techniques for the Magus*. Translated by Guido Stucco. Edited by Michael Moynihan. Rochester, VT: Inner Traditions, 2001.

Faustus, Sir. *Liber Ars Collegium*. 2001.

Faustus, Sir. "To Be a Guildsman." *Grail Stone* 1 (2002).

Guénon, René. *The Crisis of the Modern World*. Translated by Marco Pallis, Arthur Osborne, and Richard C. Nicholson. Hillsdale, NY: Sophia Perennis, 2001.

Guénon, René. *The Reign of Quantity and the Signs of the Times*. Translated by Lord Northbourne. Hillsdale, NY: Sophia Perennis, 2001.

Order of the Trapezoid. <trapezoid.org>.

Rune-Guild. <rune-gild.org>.

Temple of Set. <xeper.org>.

Westcoat, Eirik. "Runes for the Grails: Creating Old English Rune Poem Stanzas for Cweorð, Calc, Stān, and Gār." In *Eagle's Mead*, 249–89, 178–82 (poem translation). Long Branch, PA: Skaldic Eagle Press, 2019.

Wolfram von Eschenbach. *Parzival and Titurel*. Translated by Cyril Edwards. Oxford: Oxford University Press, 2006.

The Quartets of the Elder Futhark and Anglo-Saxon Futhorc: A Sixfold of Creation, Society, Nature, Cosmos, Divinity, and World

Introduction

Most of my readers will be familiar with the organization of the Elder Futhark into ættir (families) of eight runes each. Some popular authors today have attempted to make explicit delineations of the meanings of each ætt and how the runes relate to the theme of their ætt. Chris Travers does this in a more prose expository manner, whereas D. Jonathan Jones channels it through poetry.[1] Each sees the ættir as corresponding to Dumezil's three functions, but in a different order. That the runes in the Elder Futhark also have a strong pairwise correspondence is also widely known, and it is best and most elegantly explicated in a short piece by Edred Thorsson titled "Runic Dyads."[2]

However, there have not been many efforts to relate the runes to the quartets they are in, inside the standard Futhark order. Elmer Seebold does make a try at quartets, but leaves it incomplete, as many of the names are too uncertain to draw secure conclusions in an academic work. However, he does suggest that the scheme could be a threefold of living beings, nature, and social environment, with each group having two different quartets.[3] Here, I will attempt to explicate the themes of each of the six quartets in order, daring for more precision than Seebold did, and offer esoteric interpretations that can be used for magical or self-development purposes. One might also glean new divinatory aspects from this, although that is not the aim.

Note that everything just said also holds true for the first three ættir of the Anglo-Saxon Futhorc as well. Indeed, the Anglo-Saxon runic sources, especially the Old English Rune Poem

---

[1] Travers, *The Serpent and the Eagle*; Jones, *Three Paths through Midgard*.

[2] Edred, *ALU*, 197–202.

[3] Seebold, "Was Haben," 539.

(hereafter OERP) are crucial to reconstructing what we have of the Elder Futhark tradition and its ættir and quartets. Therefore, this essay will draw on those Anglo-Saxon sources and aim to be applicable for a quartet-based approach to the Anglo-Saxon Futhorc and the OERP. This will stand on its own, but it is also meant as groundwork for a companion piece in which I will explicate the three triads of the fascinating fourth ætt of the Anglo-Saxon Futhorc.[4]

Clarifications of Time and Futharks

My analysis will attempt to impose a mythic ordering on the Elder Futhark. It must be remembered that if such an ordering actually existed, it would be based on the mythology of the Germanic peoples at the time of the creation of the Elder Futhark. Mythologies change over time, and that of the Germanic peoples would be no exception. Therefore, it will be necessary to make some reasoned speculations about how things may have plausibly changed over the millennia. The exact time at issue is hard to pin down. If one takes the beginning of runic writing as the beginning of the runic tradition, as is usual among many scholars today, then it is roughly the start of the common era. Elsewhere, I argue that the runic tradition existed in a purely oral-poetic form for quite some time before runic writing, putting its start at perhaps 500 BCE at the earliest.[5] The sources for our knowledge of the mythology are very much later, the bulk of it being close to 1000–1250 CE, give or take, in the form of sagas, eddas, and rune poems. But there are a few sources, such as Tacitus, which are much closer to the origins of the Futhark. Ultimately, while the mythology at the time of the adoption of the Futhark would surely be different from that of the Old Norse, we can nevertheless still see the rough outlines quite clearly and speak meaningfully about what the gaps are and what may have filled them.

The OERP, which will be a major factor here, is generally dated to the eighth or ninth century. It preserved all of the twenty-four original runes from the Elder Futhark, and it is the primary

---

[4] See the essay immediately following in this volume.

[5] Westcoat, "The Mysteries before Rune-Staves."

poetic source for the eight runes that do not have descendants in the Old Icelandic or Old Norwegian Rune Poems (hereafter OIRP and ONRP). For an excellent scholarly resource on the OERP, I recommend *The Old English Rune Poem: A Critical Edition*, by Maureen Halsall.

In addition, the seeker would be well served by obtaining another text, *The Rune Poems: A Reawakened Tradition*, edited by P. D. Brown and Michael Moynihan. Not only does it have translations and original language texts of the various traditional rune poems, it also has modern rune poems written by a variety of seekers. Whatever the source, I recommend having a copy of the OERP on hand if you need it, since this essay will assume a working knowledge of it, as well as a decent general knowledge of the Elder Futhark itself and its esoteric qualities, such as one might find in *Runelore* by Edred Thorsson (or the aforementioned book by Chris Travers).

The six quartets of the Futhark, as I see them, have the following themes, in order: creation, society, nature, cosmos, divinity, and world. I will now walk through each quartet in turn. In doing so, I will justify these views and discuss the practical applications of these groupings, which means their usefulness for meditation, initiatory development, and operative workings.

First Quartet: Creation

Fehu, Ūruz, Þurisaz, and Ansuz constitute the quartet of creation. Specifically, I see them as an early Germanic version of the Old Norse creation myth. Fehu—although domestic cattle, gold, or wealth later—is probably here a kind of cosmic fire of creation, of unbridled energy. A reflection of this is found in the later OIRP kennings, which have Fé, in its capacity as gold, kenned as "fire of the flood tide," revealing the connection of this rune to fire. Here, it calls to mind the mixing of fire from Muspellsheim and ice from Niflheim in the middle of Ginnungagap at the start of creation. Ūruz is clearly wild cattle (aurochs), and as such, it would refer to Aðumbla, the primordial bovine in the creation myth, who is necessarily wild as the very first animal in existence, with no one yet to domesticate her. Aðumbla licks on the primal salt-ice block, releasing from it the first proto-god, Búri, who is one of Óðinn's grandfathers. Þurisaz, as a kind of thurs or giant, corresponds to Ymir, the primal being created along with Aðumbla from the first mixing of fire and ice in Ginnungagap. Ansuz, as is well known, is the rune of Óðinn, as revealed by the kennings for the rune in the OIRP and the description given in the OERP. Óðinn is the creator god who finishes the initial work of creation by sacrificing Ymir and creating Yggdrasil and the Nine Worlds from his body. These correspondences give this quartet an archetypal quality. The quartet can also be seen as the deep treasures of the unconscious: the gold of Fehu, the drinking horn of Ūruz, the hammer of Þurisaz, and furious wode of Ansuz.

In the OERP, Feoh leads off this quartet and the Futhorc with a message encouraging generosity with one's wealth, even as wealth is recognized as a comfort. This is true of various non-material kinds of wealth, such as the spiritual. This could be a faint echo of the circulation of the primal fire of Fehu in the creation myth. The Ūr strophe then advocates that one be bold and courageous in one's action, and prepared to fight if necessary. It is still clearly wild cattle, the aurochs, so the connection to Aðumbla is still there. The Þorn strophe warns of the dangers one encounters in thorns, in both the active manner of grasping and the passive manner of stopping to rest among them. It is some distance from Þurisaz, but the element of danger is still firmly in place. Ōs, as both Wōden and Mouth, finishes with an emphasis on speaking, wisdom, comfort, and that when it is used properly, this brings hope and happiness to the noble ones. Here, the connection to Ansuz still comes through clearly.

On a deeper initiatory level, the elder quartet represents the plan by which one brings into manifestation the desired things in one's life, especially via magical workings. Use the first four runes as an invocation for creating anything, whether a change in your circumstances or a work of art. They are also a tool for meditating on the creation myth to further glean its mysteries. The OERP quartet is similar, but with slightly different flavors: the circulation of energy, boldness and ferocity, advice to wield it carefully and avoid grasping (getting stuck in over-attachment or obsession), and to speak one's will with wisdom, hope, happiness, and the craft of Wōden. Thus it is also a guide to manifestation and creation.

Second Quartet: Society

Raiðō, Kiznaz,[6] Gebō, and Wunjō constitute the quartet of society. Everything here is human and social, in a pair pertaining to concrete technology and a pair pertaining to concepts in the social order. Raiðō is wagon and riding, a human-created means of traveling farther and faster. It is human know-how applied to the animal world in channeling the horse for its power. Kiznaz is the pine torch, the mastery of fire put to human ends to create light for human use. As such, it also represents the various other human uses of fire: for blacksmithing, heating, cooking, and cremation. (Remember that Fehu is more the cosmic fire of creation, one that has not been domesticated for human use.) It is human know-how applied to the plant world in channeling trees for the energy they contain. More broadly, it is human ingenuity and developing one's talents for the betterment of self and society. We may see the pair of Raiðō and Kiznaz as the solar wagon and its fire. (See the fourth quartet below for the greater importance of the sun to the early Germanics.) Gebō as gift represents exchange between humans and is thus literally the fundamental basis of society. Without it, cooperation is impossible. Gifts are what keep the completely destitute or injured alive in society so that they may have a chance to return to full participation when they are whole. Wunjō is joy, the most abstract concept in the Futhark, and yet one of the most critical. It is joy that keeps a human society motivated and healthy, and joy is the result of Gebō's exchanges functioning properly.

On the deeper initiatory level, Raiðō is the wagon of self that is prepared through careful work: physical training, meditation, and so forth. Kiznaz is the inner fire of desire that sustains one through the long process of that self-transformation, and the creativity that it brings out. Gebō is the gift of self to Self to win

---

[6] Some of the rune name forms I use here, such as Kiznaz, may not be familiar to my readers. In various recent academic sources, the reconstructions for some of the Proto-Germanic rune names are different from what readers may be familiar with in *Runelore* by Edred Thorsson.

the runes, which results in the transcendent joy of Wunjō. This is notable because it is a common modern tradition that joy is a significant characteristic of Óðinn, despite his often grim appearances otherwise. Also, as a result of their connection to that initiatory process, these four runes may correspond to the personal, inner "society."

In the OERP, we have social advice for interacting with one's fellows and relating to society. The Rād strophe warns us that while action seems easy to the one drinking in the mead hall, it is often much more difficult and unpleasant to be out there in the world actually going through with it. The Cēn strophe exemplifies an ideal public persona, equating it with the technology of the torch—to be clear, bright, and known by one's fire (=charisma, drive, focus), and that this is often most visible when noble ones are gathered together in a hall. Gyfu reminds us of the necessity and boon of exchanges, and that gifting is essential to have a society where everyone is taken care of, including travelers and the poor. And the Wynn strophe clarifies the proper attitude for obtaining joy so that all this can work properly: keeping troubles, pains, and sorrows to their proper number while having power, blessedness, and a good enough home. After all, those who are homeless are the ones most in need of gifts, and least likely to be able to give gifts themselves.

Invoke this quartet for integrating yourself into a social grouping: the need to travel to see friends (as advised by *Hávamál* 34) and interact with your fellows, developing your own special talent and craft that you can use to enrich your life and the society around you, the giving of gifts to build networks of trust and reciprocity, and the attitude of magnanimous joy that keeps the process well-grounded and working properly. Alternatively, invoke it for progress in your journey of self-transformation and giving self to Self by following Óðinn's example. The OERP quartet's flavor here is also related, but different. It advises moderation and measurement in one's thoughts and judgments of others, the inner and outward noble bearing to aspire to, the necessity of gift-giving, and the aspiration to joy that holds it all together.

Third Quartet: Nature

Quite clearly, the third quartet of Hagalaz, Nauðiz, Ísa, and Jára is first and foremost about nature and the outdoor realms that are not shielded from the elements like the space inside the home. Hagalaz is the most violent of these as hail, which was much more of an ever-present threat in the Nordic regions.[7] Esoterically, Hagalaz represents any kind of sudden adversity that issues from outside the self. Nauðiz, as need, is the most internal of this quartet, as it refers to the qualitatively human experience of constraint, adverse nature, and circumstances. The stave form is suggestive of the need-fire, kindled by creating friction between the proverbial two sticks. The stave is thus a guide to dealing with the impact of nature as a whole. Ísa is ice, and it can represent treacherous danger: the ancient Germanics would find it useful to cross in many cases, but it needed to be tested carefully to make sure it was firm, or death could result. It is also the stillness that winter brings, when the crops have been brought in for the season and one must wait many months before planting anew. It is the cold that kills any remaining unharvested crops, and puts all of the deciduous trees to sleep for the winter, and slows down the conifers, even if they do not lose their leaves. Esoterically, Ísa represents a "freezing" and stillness of all metaphorical kinds. Jára is the harvest, and the warm and bright times of the year that bring it. It governs the planting and growing of crops, and their proper tending in order to reap a bountiful harvest. In Jára, one learns the lesson of the harvest, of proper planting and caring for crops over a long period of time, which includes making contingencies for the natural disasters associated with the three preceding runes. Esoterically, it is these lessons applied to any long-term process that can be analogized to the harvest. Writing a book, improving one's skills, and building muscle are just a few examples of processes that have Jára aspects in this sense. The mastery of this quartet thus represents a general mastery of the natural world. Not in the modern sense of subduing it and eliminating its naturalness (think Heidegger's *Bestand* here, for

---

[7] In the part of Pennsylvania where I have lived most of my life, hail is rather infrequent and seldom of much consequence.

those who are familiar with it), but of a multi-faceted approach of acceptance, transformation, work-arounds, and so forth, for each aspect of nature as is most appropriate. These four runes are eminently runes of physicality in a manner much stronger than the other quartets. Esoterically, the initiatory lesson here is about confronting, adapting to, and using natural forces and cycles of all kinds.

The OERP strophes also emphasize the nature connection and give very precise messages about dealing with these elements of nature. The Hægl strophe emphasizes the source of hail in the mysterious workings of the heavens, its white color associated with purity in the Christian-influenced worldview of this poem. It also emphasizes its brevity—wind may hurl it about causing harm, but it melts and turns to water nonetheless. The Nȳd strophe emphasizes the constraint that it brings, but that it can inspire ingenuity, action, or some other kind of salvation if it is listened carefully to. The Īs strophe emphasizes the great danger of ice that is paired with its great beauty—the world of nature is often like that, both beautiful and dangerous at the same time, and we must remember that. The Gēr strophe brings harvest, and in the Christianization of this poem, the action of it is attributed to deity. But that harvest is really a natural law, and not a moral one, is shown by the last line, in that the earth's gifts go to both rich and poor.

Invoke this quartet for a mastery of the natural world—not in the sense of dominating it, but rather in proper harmonious integration with it, so that it supports your life as best as possible. The struggle against adverse conditions, with the benefit of the need fire to overcome stasis—or to know when to rest—and reach the goal of harvest. In a sense, the whole quartet finds its fulfillment in the harvest with Jāra. Those are also its lessons on an outer level, living and working with the natural environment. They are also its lessons on the inner level: transforming yourself through initiatory work, struggling against adversity, fueled by inner desire and rebellion against constraint, and knowing how to properly alternate cycles of stillness and action. The OERP strophes are focused primarily on the outward aspects: enduring adversity while knowing that it is temporary and will pass, listening to the wisdom to be found in constraining situations, and appreciating the beauty of nature while heeding its dangers, all while remaining hopeful for the goal of harvest.

Fourth Quartet: Cosmos

With Æhwaz, Perþrō, Algiz (or Elhaz), and Sōwilō, we have a quartet that represents the cosmic order arranged by Óðinn after he slew Ymir. Æhwaz is the World Tree, Yggdrasil. The name Perþrō seems to mean either pear tree or the name of a lost ancient Germanic game or both. As both, it makes much sense. It is the working of wyrd through games of chance and thus all hidden mechanisms of what we might characterize as random probability or hidden causes. It calls to mind the Well of Wyrd because of a peculiar fact: pear trees are able to grow and thrive in very moist conditions, even standing water. These trees are thus signs of hidden water under the ground and hidden circumstances in the unseen realms. Algiz may have a couple of potential meanings and possibly different forms of the name which fit here. As Elhaz, it is the elk, and calls to mind the four harts that nibble on the leaves of Yggdrasil, or the hart Eikþyrnir who also nibbles on the World Tree, with the result that dew from his horns drops down into Hvergelmir, one of the three wells under the roots of Yggdrasil. If the swan possibility for the rune is pursued, it calls to mind the two swans that feed in the Well of Wyrd. We see thus far this quartet clearly relates to the cosmology of the World Tree and its ecosystem. The final rune of the quartet is Sōwilō. It is the sun that shines down upon the whole system. From the surviving mythology, it is not as clearly related or integrated into the cosmic ecosystem, so it is necessary to postulate a lost connection to the other three that dates back to Proto-Germanic times. The sun very likely did have a larger role in the mythology, reflected by its prominence in the early Gotlandic picture stones. But such a larger role appears to have been discarded in the aftermath of the 536 CE dust veil event, perhaps the result of volcanic eruptions creating enough atmospheric dust to dim the sun. People all over the world recorded that the sun seemed to shine less brightly, as if being in a constant state of partial eclipse. This also correlates with a sharp decline in sun imagery on those Gotlandic picture stones.

The sun failed the people in a major way, and it thus lost its once exalted place in Germanic mythology. Today, however, we might consider reviving a more prominent place for the sun.

In the OERP, we have the majority of the scant evidence for the meaning of some of these runes. The Ēoh strophe makes clear that this is a yew tree, and it notes some significant attributes: that it is firmly rooted in the earth, that it is the keeper of fire, and that it is a joy on an estate, giving it a significant link to the Ēðel strophe. The Peorð strophe gives us the only concrete description of what the rune is, for we are not even sure of the meaning of the name. I take the view that the name refers to a game of some kind (now lost) which likely had an element of chance—one of several perfectly reasonable interpretations of the strophe. This connects it to the workings of wyrd. So too might the beer hall reference, and the word in the first line, *symble* (always) would also call to mind its homophone, *symble* (*symbel*, "feast" in the dative case), the drinking ceremony where the participants shape wyrd through significant speech. The Eolh strophe is another unusual one. The rune itself is Eolh, and in the manuscript it is represented by that rune. However, the stanza is about a compound, *Eolh-secg*, and the *secg* part is written out in Latin letters like the rest of the strophe. It harks back to the Þorn strophe in mentioning something dangerous to grasp. Its thriving in watery places brings an interesting twist, as does the fact that *eolhsecg* is a kenning for a sword in addition to the name of some water plant. The Sigel strophe is about the sun, but curiously focuses on sailors' attitudes toward it and its necessity while on long sea voyages. A strong link to the Lagu strophe is made by their both using *brimhengest* (brine stallion) as a kenning for a ship. But in any case, the OERP does not preserve a strong cosmos aspect for this quartet.

The quartet is one of the contrasts of the vertical axis of the world—the Well of Wyrd and the roots of Yggdrasil run deep, but the horns of the hart point upward, and the sun is highest of all. Invoke this quartet for any kind of journey-work into the realms of Yggdrasil, to orient yourself to the Tree, the Well, their Beings, and the Sun that shines over all of them. Also for when you seek greater knowledge of the totality of existence that is expressed in this model. These four runes make an excellent shorthand for the whole of the cosmos. The flavor of the OERP quartet is a bit different. Invoke it for adventuring of various kinds: Ēoh is the sturdy tree of the passionate-at-heart adventuring, setting out to test the odds and seek the unknown in Peorð, who must travel in dark places and be wary of the danger where Eolhsecg lurks, all the while keeping Sigel as a guide until he has come home again.

Fifth Quartet: Divinity

In Tīwaz, Berkanō, Ehwaz, and Mannaz, we have a quartet of gods. This is more obvious in the first pairing with Tiwaz and Berkanō. There is no doubt about the divinity of Tīwaz. Berkanō, however, is more concealed. But as a word, it contains the *-an-* infix denoting a master or leader of something, just as Wōðanaz is the master of the inspired ones. In this case, Berkanō would be the mistress of birch, especially since Berkanō > ON Bjarkan is not the ordinary word for birch. That would be **berkō* > ON *björk*. In any event, it is clear that a goddess Berkanō did not later retain the status that the Proto-Germanic implies that she had, as the OERP and OIRP verses clearly have the word meaning an ordinary tree. (And OE *beorc* does not retain any remnants of that *-an-* infix.) With Ehwaz and Mannaz, the divinity connection is more by mythological allusion rather than direct statement. Ehwaz would have called to mind divinities and heroes strongly associated with horses, especially those descended from the Proto-Indo-European "Divine Twins," of which there are many, such as the later Hengist and Horsa among the Saxons and the Asvins of the Vedic culture. The Proto-Germanics had theirs as well, of which the main trace is the twin deities called the Alcis, as mentioned in Tacitus. There is even the possibility that the rune name could have originally been *Ehwō in the dual form of the noun, which would literally mean "the two horses." But over time, as the importance of these gods diminished, replacement of the name by the ordinary singular in line with the rest of the rune names would have occurred. (The technical linguistics term for that is *analogical leveling*.) For Mannaz, the mythological link would be the deity Mannus, again mentioned by Tacitus, which implies a Proto-Germanic of *Mannuz. This may be the same root, just with a different stem vowel and declension, but even if it is not, the folk etymology of the time would likely see the one as an allusion to the other. This Mannus was considered the progenitor god of three different early Germanic tribes, and Mannus had three sons, each corresponding to one of the tribes.

In all these cases, it is clear that the nature of the religion changed, and so did the status of these divinities, who were reduced in importance or lost. In the case of Tīwaz, the scholarly speculations—that he once had a larger cult as potentially the high god of the pantheon who got supplanted by Óðinn—are well known. Berkanō, too, is unknown in later times, but thematically, we might wonder if she got absorbed by Freyja or Frigg—or that one of those two originally had that name. For the Alcis, it is the same, though one can speculate whether they were absorbed by or transformed into Njörðr and his unnamed sister (one or both from the root *Nerþuz, who appears in Tacitus as Nerthus), or Freyr and Freyja, or some amalgamation of three of them (here, one might be reminded of the PIE Divine Twins who had a sister or wife in common). In any event, only the later Hengist and Horsa of the Saxons are a clear, divine-horse-twins analog among the later Germanics. Mannus, however he may have been associated with the rune, is also a deity who clearly did not survive under that name, whatever may have happened to him.

In any event, we have a solid quartet here—four gods, or a god, goddess, and the most important living beings of the society that honors them, horse and man. Esoterically, this quartet speaks of a right and harmonious relationship between these beings. Tīwaz as sky god, Berkanō as earth goddess, horses as the direct conduit to the gods (Tacitus again, in his mention that the Germanic priests held horses sacred for divinatory purposes), and Mannus as the progenitor of the society. And here, even if we do not consider all four runes to represent gods, it is clear enough that the latter three greatly partake of the divine, including humans who were specifically gifted a divine nature by Óðinn-Vili-Vé.

The OERP strophes for these runes have, like the names themselves, gotten very far away from any kind of discourse about deities. The Tir strophe has no mention of the god and is instead about a star or other celestial body, one that serves as a faithful, never-failing guide during the nighttime. The Beorc strophe emphasizes the abundant life energy of the tree, its beauty, and its reaching toward the sky—earth is only present implicitly here. The Eh strophe emphasizes the nobility of the horse. It is most interesting that there are three words for horse used in this strophe, and four words for noblemen. The Man strophe emphasizes how human companionship is essential for all of us, and the brevity of life and the inevitability of death.

Invoke this quartet for interactions with the gods, especially as a whole—under my four-gods interpretation, these runes are a shorthand for the Germanic pantheon as a whole, but an early version that may have more differences from the later Old Norse than we suspect. Or, in a not-four-gods approach, invoke it for right order among the beings of the world, where god, tree, horse, and human are a shorthand for all living creatures. Use an OERP-based invocation for a short-hand guide to life in Midgard: guidance from the stars through Tir, reaching toward the sky with Beorc, finding an excellent partner by Eh, and always taking joy in one's fellow Man.

Sixth Quartet: World

The final quartet of Laguz, Ingwaz, Dagaz, and Ōþala may be seen as ideal life in the world. It contrasts nicely with the fourth quartet —while that quartet was about the grand scheme of the cosmos in a total, unifying way, this quartet is the ideal world experienced by the living human. There is the water of oceans, lakes, and rivers found in Laguz; the fertile earth represented by Ingwaz; the shining day that benefits everyone in Dagaz; and finally, one's ancestral homeland at the center and end of it all with Ōþala.

The OERP strophes for these runes can be looked at as a group. In them, there is much concern over land, sea, and day. In the Lagu strophe, we have the endlessness of the sea, and the uncertainty of voyages on it, and the implicit ever-present hope for returning to land. The land and sea dichotomy is continued with the Ing strophe, which is made explicit in Ing's coming from across the waves and returning there, as well as the mention of his wagon for the land-side element. The Dæg strophe emphasizes the universality of day, in its usefulness to all, and that all know it comes from the Drighten and the Measurer (= Wōden and Tīw, by following the pre-Christian implications of the wording). The Ēðel strophe gives us the blessedness of the good life: an ancestral home, prosperity, and adherence to tradition. There is an implied yew on this estate, further implying connection to the right order of cosmos (that is, the estate situated in right relation to the totality of the World Tree), via the explicit mention of Ēðel in the Ēoh strophe. On the basis of the Ing strophe, one may see a kind of hero's journey motif in these four runes.

Invoke this quartet as a charm for manifesting the good life around you: water nearby and plenty to drink, fertile earth and food from it, the shining sky to illuminate everything, and a secure estate on which to prosper and enjoy all this.[8] More ambitiously, invoke this to bring that good life to the people around you. This quartet is a shorthand for a proper, harmonious existence in the world. In this age of changing climates, resource depletion, exploitive economies, mono-crop agriculture, and so forth that leads to increased poverty and precarity, this quartet represents the life we should strive to make available to all. Invoke the OERP runes for a similar, but slightly different theme: that Lagu, Ing, Dæg, and Ēðel are kept in harmonious relationship in your life— or a kind of hero's journey to cross the "sea" and bring back "day" to one's home.

Conclusion

As the six quartets make up the whole Futhark, their themes must, of course, add up to a totality of some kind. In that regard, creation, society, nature, cosmos, divinity, and world do fit together as a whole. They are a six-fold of existence. That is, six different modes in the totality of humanity's existence in the universe. As a whole, they can be invoked for greater knowledge of our place in existence and how the worlds fit together. And it provides a new way of looking at the entire 24-rune Futhark as a formula of right order and wholeness.

For even more possible ways to relate to the quartets, one should work through the curriculum of *The Nine Doors of*

---

[8] To me, this quartet feels a bit like a Proto-Germanic version of Heidegger's Fourfold, very loosely speaking.

Midgard. Through the core Rune-Thinking exercises, one can internalize the runes and gain further insights into the nature of the quartets. And through the Yew Work and Road Wending exercises, one relates the quartets to the various pathways among Yggdrasil, which provides further keys for using these quartets in meditation and operative workings. It is these exercises, along with my academic study, that I credit for preparing my bold synthesis here in this essay.

For a long time, the importance of the runic dyads and the individual ættir has been recognized. Now, the quartets can have their due as the proper bridge between dyad and ætt. May it lead to the Runers out there discovering further mysteries. Reyn til Rúna!

Works Cited

Brown, P. D., and Michael Moynihan, eds. *The Rune Poems: A Reawakened Tradition.* North Augusta, SC: Gilded Books, 2022.

Edred Thorsson. *ALU: An Advanced Guide to Operative Runology.* San Francisco: Weiser, 2012.

Edred Thorsson. *The Nine Doors of Midgard: A Curriculum of Rune-work.* 5th ed. Moss Beach, CA: The Rune-Gild, 2016.

Edred Thorsson. *Runelore: A Handbook of Esoteric Runology.* Boston: Weiser, 1987.

Halsall, Maureen. *The Old English Rune Poem: A Critical Edition.* McMaster Old English Studies and Texts 2. Toronto: University of Toronto Press, 1981.

Jones, D. Jonathan. *Three Paths through Midgard: A Rune Poem.* Portland, OR: RavensHalla Arts, 2010.

Larrington, Carolyne, trans. *The Poetic Edda.* 2nd ed. Oxford: Oxford University Press, 2014.

Seebold, Elmar. "Was haben die Germanen mit den Runen gemacht? Und wieviel haben sie davon von ihren antiken Vorbildern gelernt?" In *Germanic Dialects: Linguistic and Philological Investigations,* edited by Bela Brogyanyi and Thomas Krömmelbein, 525–83. Amsterdam: John Benjamins Publishing, 1986.

Snorri Sturluson. *Edda*. Translated by Anthony Faulkes. London: Everyman, 1987.

Tacitus. *The Agricola and the Germania*. Translated by H. Mattingly and revised by S. A. Handford. Baltimore: Penguin Books, 1970.

Travers, Chris. *The Serpent and the Eagle: An Introduction to the Elder Runic Tradition*. 2009.

Westcoat, Eirik. "The Mysteries before Rune-Staves: Explaining Futhark Order and Rune Names via an Ur-Poem Prior to Runic Writing." Forthcoming.

Westcoat, Eirik. "Runes for the Grails: Creating Old English Rune Poem Stanzas for Cweorð, Calc, Stān, and Gār." In *Eagle's Mead*, 249–89, 178–82 (poem translation). Long Branch, PA: Skaldic Eagle Press, 2019.

The Fourth Ætt of the Anglo-Saxon Futhorc: Triads of Initiation, Knighthood, and Mastery

Introduction

Following from my preceding piece on the quartets of the Elder Futhark and Anglo-Saxon Futhorc, it is time to address the mysterious final ætt of the Anglo-Saxon Futhorc. Oddly, it consists of nine runes, instead of the usual eight, at its fullest extent. (Unless you wish to think of the final rune as in a fifth ætt all by itself, an approach that may also reveal some mysteries.) Since all of its rune names are novel creations of the Anglo-Saxons and do not have predecessors in the Elder or Younger Futhark—with perhaps one exception—this discussion will generally be limited to the evidence of the Old English Rune Poem (hereafter OERP) and some general material on those runes from Edred Thorsson. And here, I am not making any claims as to how the Anglo-Saxons saw this ætt of the Futhorc, but rather about the uses it can be put to today, particularly from an initiatory perspective. In furtherance of that, I will take a leap and build on one of my prior esoteric creations, "Runes for the Grails." That is a long essay featuring an eleven-line poem in Old English I wrote to give strophes to the runes of Cweorð, Calc, Stān, and Gār, which were included in a list of thirty-three Anglo-Saxon runes in the Cotton Library manuscript. That manuscript was the sole source for the OERP, which only has strophes for the first twenty-nine runes, leaving those final four without poetry. And so I wrote my strophes to ameliorate that deficiency—more on that later.

As with the immediately preceding article, this piece assumes a working knowledge of the OERP, at least the historical strophes, and so again, I recommend *The Old English Rune Poem: A Critical Edition* by Maureen Halsall as a scholarly resource on it. The seeker would also be well served again by *The Rune Poems: A Reawakened Tradition*, edited by P. D. Brown and Michael Moynihan. As for the strophes associated with Cweorð, Calc, Stān, and Gār, those are my creation, but of course I discuss those strophes much more in depth in my essay "Runes for the Grails" in my book *Eagle's Mead*.[1]

Regarding the initiatory perspective, I will consider the two initiatory systems I am most familiar with. The first is the Rune-Gild, of which I have been an initiate since late 2011, and am currently a Master as of the time I'm writing this. The Rune-Gild has three main initiatory levels (or degrees, if you will): Learner, Fellow, and Master, which are meant to correspond to the most traditional system of three degrees found in craft guilds: apprentice, journeyman, and master. One sees an analogous system also in Freemasonry, with the degrees of Entered Apprentice, Fellow Craft, and Master Mason. The second initiatory system is that of the once-and-future Guild of the Grail, mentioned in other essays in this volume. It was a short-lived Traditionalist initiatory Order that emerged in the early 2000s, which I had first discovered only after it was long defunct. It applied the three-degree system to the model of knighthood, and originally called those degrees Guildsman, Esquire, and Knight (which is what you'll see if you happen to find the old public documents from that Order somewhere online).[2] Here, I have opted for a traditional restoration by calling those degrees Page, Squire, and Knight, hearkening back to the medieval times when the first two were steps on the path of training to be a knight.

The Runes of the Fourth Ætt

The runes of the fourth ætt and the basic meanings of their names are as follows:
- Āc 'Oak'
- Æsc 'Ash'
- Ȳr 'Yew Bow'
- Īar 'Serpent'?
- Ēar 'Earth Grave'
- Cweorð 'Fire-Bore'?
- Calc 'Chalice'

---

[1] Westcoat, "Runes for the Grails," 249–89, 178–82 (poem translation).

[2] Sir Faustus, *Liber Ars Collegium*.

- Stān 'Stone'
- Gār 'Spear'

The question marks are to indicate that the meaning of the name is uncertain. Those two words seem to be *hapax legomena* in Old English, with the result that the poetic stanza attached to Īar is our only clue to its meaning, and comparative etymology is the only guide for Cweorð. Not a great situation to be in, but we must try our best with it. Edred has a lore chapter covering the basics about them and their names.[3] It is Ȳr that appears related to the Younger Futhark rune name Ýr, which also means yew bow and would be pronounced quite similarly, if not the same, in both languages. Michael Barnes suggests rather that Ȳr is a meaningless name created by analogy with Ūr, from which it seems reasonable to claim phonetic derivation due to i-mutation.[4] While the sound is indeed an i-mutation of /u/, the poetic strophe clearly does not treat the name as meaningless. Borrowing the name's meaning from Old Norse, which had the same kind of vowel resulting from an i-mutation of /u/, seems as reasonable a possibility as any other, one which helps us make better sense of its poetic strophe, which would otherwise be obscure. The other eight names are not seen as rune names in any other system.

The First Triad: Preparedness and Virtues

This triad is filled with notions of preparedness, training, and virtues. All three of the names of the triad are trees: Oak, Ash, and Yew (Bow). In Oak, we see its practicality emphasized: through acorns, it provides food for the meat animals we consume, and through its wood, it can be made into ships. But while the final lines of the strophe appear to be about how the sea will test how seaworthy the ship is, they are also a hidden reference to the human being who is tested by the sea, since names of trees are often used as *heiti* for human beings. And so the sea tests whether the sailor has noble troth: will he face the challenges faithfully, stay the course for the voyage and show his endurance, or will he become frightened and desert at the next port of call?

---

[3] Edred, *ALU*, 126–43.

[4] Barnes, *Runes: A Handbook*, 39.

The Ash strophe is less circumspect about its metaphors. While its first half is in praise of the arboreal entity, the latter half can only be talking about a human warrior. After all, what tree could possibly be said to hold its place even though fought against by many people? Here, this speaks of the virtues of steadfastness, perseverance, duty, and warriorship. (But if we take that latter half to be about the universal World Tree itself, it suggests some rather peculiar mysteries to explore about just who are the many people fighting against it!) Finally, the Yew Bow strophe does not use tree metaphors for human beings. Instead, it is straightforward in saying "it looks fine on a steed, is reliable on a journey, a kind of army-gear."[5] It is also said to be for both nobles and warriors. The bow is a means of action at a distance, of projecting lethal power to hunt animals or kill opposing warriors. And so it represents a significant enhancement to the powers of the warrior.

These strophes call for the initiate to be faithful and endure, to be steadfast and persevering in the face of opposition, to be mindful of duty, and finally to have the proper gear, something suitable for both warrior and noble, which extends his capabilities beyond himself. Esoterically, this is the work of the Page in the Guild of the Grail: cultivating these virtues and preparedness by acquiring a solid grounding in Traditionalism prior to undertaking the deep work of initiatory transformation. In the Rune-Gild, one may think of it as the work of the Learner through the early Doors of Midgard. Certainly Doors 3 and 4, running a marathon 240 days each, require those virtues to see them through! And both the Page and the Learner, once they complete their work at this level, will indeed have perspectives and capabilities beyond their former ordinary selves.

The Second Triad: Transitions

This triad is filled with transitions and liminality, as the names of these runes appear to mean Serpent, Grave, and Fire-Bore. They start out pleasant with the Īar strophe in the OERP. It is some kind of river-creature, and that's where it lives, but it is said to take its food on land. So this is an animal that frequently transitions

---

[5] Halsall, *The Old English Rune Poem*, 93.

between water and land. Nevertheless, its residence is one surrounded by water, which gives the impression that it could be an island dweller, or perhaps a beaver in its lodge (instead of a serpent). It is most important to note that it is joyful there.

The Ēar strophe then turns to the dark and grim transitions. It is the grave, and the transition of the corpse from a freshly dead warm body, to a cold body, and then finally the slow decay until only the bones are left. Memento Mori! This is portrayed as an unhappy transition, for it is said to be *egle eorla gehwylcun* "loathsome to every man."[6] Nevertheless, it is a transition we all must face one day.

The Cweorð strophe is very different. Since no strophe for the rune from the medieval period survives (that is, if a strophe ever existed, which it may not have), I chose to write one myself, in both Old English and Modern English. Why? In the Rune Realms, poetry is a strong interest of mine, and my work with the runes for magic and divination uses their poetic strophes as the most significant key to them. This led to me having a particular view: that a rune wasn't a full-fledged first-class rune unless it had a poetic strophe to go with it. And so I had to compose Old English stanzas for Cweorð, Calc, Stān, and Gār in order to properly use those runes in my Rune-Work.

For Cweorð, I followed Edred in treating the name as meaning fire-bore,[7] and having already seen the theme of transitions in both Īar and Ēar, I wrote Cweorð to provide yet another transition: the creation of fire, especially a need-fire for a funeral pyre. The cremation then releases the soul from the matter of its body to seek the higher realms. Esoterically, in Cweorð, a person applies their efforts to turn the fire-drill and produce fire, and then that fire must be turned metaphorically on themselves in order to seek spiritual development. Here, however, I must note that the cremation aspect I put into this strophe is something the original, Christian author of the OERP would not have agreed with—in fact, he would likely have been horrified, as the Old

---

[6] Halsall, *The Old English Rune Poem*, 92–93.

[7] Edred, *ALU*, 137.

English Christianity of the time considered cremation to be an extremely pagan and abhorrent practice.

Taken together, these three runes call for the initiate to take the leap out of his ordinary life and transition across the various liminal spaces. The easier transitions are started with first, those back and forth from "land" to "water," and one is reminded that cultivating joy is essential for this. Then one can go on to the more serious transitions of confronting one's mortality, followed by kindling the purifying inner fire to seek the soul's liberation. Esoterically, this is the work of the Squire in the Guild of the Grail, who embarks on the arduous journey of self-transformation through work in a traditional system of initiation. In the Rune-Gild, it is the work of the Fellow in the latter Doors of Midgard, involving much more serious steps of transformation, such as the construction of the Wode-Self and contacting one's Fetch. By the time the Squire and Fellow complete this level of the work, they will surely have faced their mortality and greatly kindled their inner fire.

The Third Triad: Grail Hallows

This is the transcendent triad of the Grail Hallows. They are Chalice, Stone, and Spear. In my interpretation of this triad, each of these is a Grail and is *the* Grail, partaking in the Germanic paradigm of significant things that occur in groups of three—it is a paradox similar to the divine triad of Óðinn-Vili-Vé. Like the Grail, each of these three is a great treasure to be sought, one that confers miraculous powers in its archetypal form. The strophes analyzed here are entirely my creation, and they strongly play up the Grail connection that Edred argued for these three runes in a brief essay titled "Grail Mythos in Old English Runes."[8] However, I have gone beyond Edred's material, most especially in connecting Stān to a specific stone.

Calc is the chalice of the Grail and the poetic mead Óðrœrir. With it, one makes operative speech during sumbel and other magical workings. My strophe emphasizes those qualities, and the crucial element of joyfulness associated with obtaining this Grail.

---

[8] Edred, *ALU*, 205–08.

Óðrœrir, and thus this rune as well, is not only the mead of poetry, but actually is poetry, and my strophe emphasizes the great value to be found in poetry, as it served as the head-ransom for the dwarves who created it. Calc is essential to the *wōðbora*, who is a bearer of wode, but also seems to be a prophet or sage in addition to a poet. As Woden quested for this Grail, so too must the seeker follow his example and quest for it also.

Stān is the heart of Hrungnir, the exemplary stone and the Germanic correspondent to the Grail stone found in Wolfram's *Parzival*, the greatest of the medieval Grail romances. It also speaks of the power to imbue stone with magic that partakes of the eternal aspects of stone to create lasting effects, such as using a well-carved rune stone to hallow a space and make it permanently holy. The end of the third line, by saying *þēos heorte eotenes* "this ettin's heart," explicitly connects it to that bravest of ettins who dared to challenge Thor to a duel, the ettin with the steadiest heart of that entire tribe of beings.[9] Hrungnir was an ettin who was made entirely of stone, and that would include his heart. And "stone" is used as a *heiti* for heart in skaldic poetry, especially a courageous one, for which Hrungnir may well have been the mythic exemplar. Via defeating Hrungnir in a duel, Thor has in some way won this most exemplary stone. And the final line of my strophe emphasizes the life-giving power of such courage and its capacity to be lasting and permanent like stone in the ideal case.

Gār is Gungnir, the spear that Woden uses to dedicate the slain to himself. It has other powers as well, against serpents in a hidden sort of way. In the "Old English Nine Herbs Charm," it is mentioned that "Then Woden grabbed the nine glory-twigs // And struck the adder so it burst into nine pieces."[10] Here, I interpret this as Woden using his spear in a special nine-fold form to smite that serpent. In my strophe, Gar represents sovereignty, first over self and then for exercising that sovereignty in the world. I emphasize that it gives three powers: "it changes the wyrd," that is, the wielder uses his power of self-sovereignty to alter his destiny according to his true will within; "it chooses the slain," that is,

---

[9] Westcoat, "Runes for the Grails," 272, 182.

[10] Williamson, *The Complete Old English Poems*, 1073.

with it, one becomes one of Woden's chosen in Valhalla; and "it summons the blood," that is, calls forth the latent inspiration in others to follow the seeker's path of initiation.[11] The final line of my strophe emphasizes the immense power of this grail and its great nobility—one becomes an aristocrat of the soul when one has mastered it.

The master of this triad is one who commands powerful and operative speech, has imbued his heart with the steadiness of Hrungnir's heart, and is sovereign over his own Tree and its nine worlds within. He is rich in the power to make himself and others holy, for each of the grails partakes of a different aspect of the hallowing powers. Esoterically, this is the work of the Knight in the Guild of the Grail, who has completed his primary training and now quests in the world to make real the grail hallows within himself as seeking the Grail has become a permanent and deeply felt duty within himself. In the Rune-Gild, it is the work of the Master who has completed the Nine Doors of Midgard, for whom Rûna is his ultimate Grail, and the runes are the key to seeking Rûna. For both Knight and Master, it reflects their power to choose Pages and Learners to teach and join in the quest of seeking the Grail and Rûna.

Conclusion: The Path of Initiation

Whether intentionally created that way or not, the fourth ætt of the Anglo-Saxon Futhorc has now been seen to offer a most intriguing set of correspondences. And it is all the more striking because the runes here fit into thematic triads, instead of quartets as was seen with the first three ættir of this Futhorc. Here, I would also emphasize my harmonious expansion of the tradition: that the first five runes fit the pattern of virtues and transitions is an objective matter of the surviving strophes, whereas with the final four runes, I have aimed to affirm that objective foundation and take it somewhere special. Hopefully, it is where the runes are trying to lead, even if ultimately it would not have been on the same path that the Anglo-Saxons would have taken for them (again, they would have been horrified by the cremation

---

[11] Westcoat, "Runes for the Grails," 182.

reference). But most importantly, in today's world, the highest and best use of the runes is for initiatory development, with magic and divination being important components of that. And here, an initiatory narrative that fits a portion of the rune row adds a new dimension of value to the treasure trove of the runic system. May initiates of the eternal Rune-Gild, the once-and-future Guild of the Grail, and other such groups that work with the Anglo-Saxon Futhorc be enriched through this synthesis of runes, initiation, and the Grail.

Works Cited

Barnes, Michael P. *Runes: A Handbook*. Woodbridge: Boydell Press, 2012.

Brown, P. D. and Michael Moynihan, eds. *The Rune Poems: A Reawakened Tradition*. North Augusta, SC: Gilded Books, 2022.

Edred Thorsson. *ALU: An Advanced Guide to Operative Runology*. San Francisco: Weiser, 2012.

Edred Thorsson. *The Nine Doors of Midgard: A Curriculum of Rune-work*. 5th ed. Moss Beach, CA: The Rune-Gild, 2016.

Halsall, Maureen. *The Old English Rune Poem: A Critical Edition*. McMaster Old English Studies and Texts 2. Toronto: University of Toronto Press, 1981.

Faustus, Sir. *Liber Ars Collegium*. 2001.

Westcoat, Eirik. "Runes for the Grails: Creating Old English Rune Poem Stanzas for Cweorð, Calc, Stān, and Gār." In *Eagle's Mead*, 249–89, 178–82 (poem translation). Long Branch, PA: Skaldic Eagle Press, 2019.

Williamson, Craig, trans. *The Complete Old English Poems*. Philadelphia: University of Pennsylvania Press, 2017.

Triadic Experiences for my Triple Quests: Examining Revelatory Singularities on My Esoteric Path

Introduction

Those reading this book, especially if you have already read my *Eagle's Mead*, may be aware that I am dedicated to three esoteric quests: the Mead (that is, poetry), the Runes, and the Grails. For each of these quests, I have had what I would call a defining mystical experience, and this essay is about those experiences. It is my hope that my discussion of them will help others who are seeking to have their own such experiences—although they should keep in mind that theirs will not be exactly like mine or anyone else's. Fortunately, there is a framework in which these experiences can be contextualized, and it is the one in which the first of those experiences occurred for me. That is the Rûna-Experience as described by Edred Thorsson, founder of the Rune-Gild. I will start with that one first, proceed to the other two, and then discuss how I analyze and generalize the concept. I will also discuss various key points of my initiatory development along the way. I will end with a description of a more recent and different sort of experience, one that points to my future at press time.

The Concept of the Rûna-Experience

One of the most influential authors in my life, Edred Thorsson, recounted the mystical experience that set him upon the path of seeking the mysteries, which would lead him to eventually found the Rune-Gild in late 1980, and later on to one of the highest and most distinguished degrees in modern Western occult initiatory systems, that of Magus (which is called Erulian in the Rune-Gild) with his formal utterance of the Word Rûna in 1988. That early experience was hearing Rûna in 1974, in a fairly unexpected moment during an afternoon car ride, and it was not from any human speaker.[1] Though it would take a long time to unfold completely (if it can ever be said to have finished unfolding), it

---

[1] Edred, *History of the Rune-Gild*, 15–17.

clearly had an immediate and profound effect on him, as he began his runic studies in earnest the very next day with a large stack of books on runes that he could find in the University of Texas library. Clearly, Edred reflected a lot on the nature of this experience, and particularly on whether others in the Rune-Gild could have analogous experiences and what that might mean for their initiatory development. And thus he describes the *Rûna-Experience*:

> Inner Rune-Work is enhanced and accelerated by something I came to call the Rûna-Experience. This experience (Icelandic *reynsla*) is a personal reflection of the way in which Óðinn received Runic knowledge in the first place. This experience may be one in which the sum total of Rune-Knowledge is at once taken into your psyche. Then the real esoteric Rune-Work can begin—that is, you begin the long and sometimes arduous task of unfolding, unraveling, learning, articulating, and giving voice to Rûna.[2]

My experience had that character. There was indeed a flash of insight, followed by the long and arduous task he describes. But Edred notes that:

> It is, however, completely unpredictable as to what the experience will be like for any individual or even what will trigger it, or how it will be perceived. The only things that are certain are that when it does happen it will be unmistakable for the individual having the experience and that it will come as a result of seeking Rûna.[3]

I had been wondering for a while if I was the sort of person who would have a Rûna-Experience and not realize it at the time. I've concluded that I was right about that. When mine occurred, I certainly recognized it as an unmistakably profound experience, but it was some time later before I realized that it warranted the label of Rûna-Experience. I should not expect my own Path and

---

[2] Edred, "*Rúnarreynsla*," online edition; I have standardized the spelling as "Rûna" in this quote and others from this source. The essay is quite short, perhaps three minutes, and you really should read it now before proceeding. There is also an out-of-print hardcopy edition, which I've listed in the works cited.

[3] Edred, "*Rúnarreynsla*," online edition.

my own Awakening to be exactly like anyone else's, maybe not even necessarily broadly similar to anyone else's. Anyway, Edred goes on to note that a lot of his material, such as the Rune-Gild's Nine Doors curriculum and various rites, is intended to facilitate having such an experience. Furthermore, he says:

> Clearly history has shown that this experience comes in two different ways: It can come in the *context*, but not necessarily the *result*, of regular disciplined exercises and studies, or it can come out of the blue with apparently no connection to any consciously anticipated cause and effect.[4]

Edred's Rûna-Experience was the latter. Mine was very definitely the former when it occurred in summer 2010. And it is time to tell of my experience, though some back story is necessary to show that it was a long time in coming.

Back Story: A Persistent Interest in Poetry and Óðrœrir

I'll start at the beginning, or at least what I think was the beginning. Around early 2006, my brother, two friends, and I were informally forming an Asatru kindred and looking for a name. In the search for a name, Óðrœrir just came to me. I don't remember the exact details of that day, or what I was doing at the time, or much anything at all. It just felt right, and it did not appear to be a name that anyone else was already using (from what I could find in a web search, but remember, the web was quite different in those days), which I thought strange, since it seemed like such a good one. But from that day, my fascination with the Mead of Poetry kept growing. Given my level of language knowledge at the time, I settled on the form "Odroerir" as it was nicely anglicized and seemed the most common. It should be noted that I did not "hear" anything in the form of sound or voice —hence, I cannot say that the Word has an exact, unalterable form. (As my knowledge of Old Norse has increased, I have used more accurate Old Norse forms, and Óðrœrir is now my preferred form.) Somewhere around this time, I got the idea that I should eventually start writing poetry for blót and sumbel, and for other

---

[4] Edred, "*Rúnarreynsla*," online edition. Italics in original.

things as well. But I did not start writing any poetry. Thought would not become action for a very long time.

During Trothmoot in June 2006, I had the revolutionary idea that the kindred shouldn't simply be *named* Óðrœrir, but rather that it should *be* an Óðrœrir kindred; that is, it should be dedicated to the Mead of Poetry and its pursuit. This would be another example of my growing fascination with the Mead. Yet still I had not tried to write any poetry! At times, I attempted to start learning the various Germanic Languages, and briefly tried to embark on the Nine Doors curriculum of the Rune-Gild, although without success. In December 2008, I even made a silver bracelet with the word Wōdhrēra on it—my attempt at an Old English cognate form written with the Anglo-Saxon Futhorc.[5] I still wear this bracelet regularly, and will continue to do so until the day it is superseded by an appropriate successor.

Not much would come of me trying to create and lead a kindred. That sort of thing takes a lot of work, and I would eventually realize that it was not the sort of work I should be doing —it would take away time and energy from the things that I Needed to be doing. And my positive experiences with the Hearth of Yggdrasil, starting in late 2010, would make it plain to me that I was much happier with other people doing the whole kindred-leading thing. In February 2009, I joined as an Associate of the Rune-Gild, and began the curriculum in the Nine Doors and *Gildisbók*. But my motivation failed, and before day 80 of Door 1, I had given up. Still I did not write any poetry. But the dreams were still there, as was the fascination with the Mead. And in January 2010, I started again on the Nine Doors curriculum. This time, I succeeded in sticking with it, and would see it through to its completion. And my fascination with the Mead continued and gained in strength.

---

[5] Though *Wōdhrēra* would be a valid construction from Old English components, if Óðrœrir had existed in Proto-Germanic, the ancestral form would have been something like *Wōþuhrōzijaz*, which would have produced possibly *Wōdhrēre* or *Wōðrǣra* in Old English.

My Own Rûna-Experience: The Reality of Óðrœrir

In June 2010, I was working through Door 2 of the Nine Doors curriculum and doing various other associated rites, such as the Rûna Working. It was then that I had my Rûna-Experience. Maybe it was during one of these workings, but probably not. I think it more likely that it was during a random moment of contemplation one of those days when I was suddenly and profoundly struck with the realization that Óðrœrir, the Mead of Poetry, was absolutely real and that it was my Task and Quest to seek, win, and pour it myself—nothing less would suffice for realizing some of my ideas about poetry. Surprisingly, I do not remember exactly when it occurred. Later that summer, in early August, it occurred to me that in my Quest, I may eventually have to Utter a Word, and most likely, that Word would be Óðrœrir.[6] Surprisingly enough, I still had not started writing any poetry, although I knew I eventually would have to.

Here, I will take brief pause in the story to point out that though Óðrœrir is a real thing that actually exists, its precise nature is mysterious. That is, it is not a physical mead that you can buy at your local liquor store! Its existence may be entirely on non-physical planes, with the potential to inhabit physical substances temporarily, with the right enchantments. It's certainly part of my quest to seek an understanding of just what it is. But I'll return to the story now, for it is not the place of this essay to address the matter of what ways Óðrœrir is real.

Later that month, at East Coast Thing, an annual Asatru festival in the Northeastern United States, a transformative surprise occurred. East Coast Thing had a tradition of lore contests, although somewhat irregularly.[7] A new form of the lore contest was introduced in 2010. Entrants would select a topic at random by rolling a die, and then have 24 hours to submit a short

---

[6] At press time, I still think this is eventually possible, but that my Word absolutely would be Óðrœrir (or possibly a cognate), and it could never be anything else, and there was never the possibility of it being anything else.

[7] As of this publication, such lore contests, regardless of form, seem to have gone completely out of style.

written work demonstrating their knowledge of the lore on that topic. It was suggested that entrants could do their submissions as poetry, short story, humor, etc. I rolled the die, got Freyr, and decided that I would try a poem, and this time, I actually wrote one! I didn't know much about poetic forms at that point, but I worked in some kennings and alliteration in haphazard fashion, and ended up with a 22-line lore poem about the life of Freyr.[8] It won second place. Finally, I had written a poem!

Later in September after ECT, I would compose and perform an early version of what became my "Óðrœrir Working."[9] (A version that didn't have any poetry in it, if you can believe that!) But somehow, I went about two months after ECT before writing any further poetry. Then, in November, I started my "Charms for the Self" poem based on my Personal Analysis Diary work (part of the Nine Doors Curriculum), and have been writing poetry regularly ever since.[10] In December 2010, I would start to use the traditional alliterative forms instead of the haphazard, improvised verse form of the charms poem. By the end of 2011, I had written several hundred stanzas in the meters of *fornyrðislag*, *ljóðaháttr*, and *galdralag*. My Rûna-Experience bore its early fruit, and I was harvesting it with vigor. One of those fruits would be another kind of experience that would occur in August 2011, and I turn to that now.

My Wode-Experience: An Encounter with the Mead Force

Having finally started writing poetry, I decided at some point near the middle of 2011 that I would have to enter, for my first time

---

[8] That poem remains unpublished as of press time. Surprisingly, I seemed to have overlooked it when preparing *Viking Poetry for Heathen Rites*. I am working on a kind of sequel to that book, with more heathen lore poems, and I have already reworked the poem into a proper alliterative form.

[9] Westcoat, *Eagle's Mead*, 165–66 and 224–25.

[10] "Charms for the Self" was an early and immature work. Its final, mature form appeared as "Staves for the Self" in Westcoat, *Eagle's Mead*, 217–23.

ever, the skaldic competition at the East Coast Thing in 2011.[11] And so I selected a poem, "The Six Treasures," from what I'd written at the time.[12] Once August 2011 rolled around, I was in Door 3 in my Rune-Work, which involved practice carvings of rune-staves, and I made quite a few at this time. I had decided that I would take a number of such carvings that I made and sacrifice them to the nightly bonfire at ECT. On Wednesday and Thursday evening, I had put a few pieces into the fire, including two practice futharks. After dinner on Friday evening, I rehearsed my poem for the skaldic competition one last time and put my final runic offerings for the evening into the main bonfire. These offerings included the third and final practice futhark I created, named Channeler, which was partly created with appropriate magical technique. I also had a practice stave with "óðr" in Younger Futhark runes that I gave to the fire with the words: "An Óðr to the fire, for Óðr from the fire!" In addition, I had a small stave with the Old English Gār rune. It was given to the fire with the words: "To the giver of ghost, a gar for Óðinn!"

Then the time came for the skaldic competition. I had been drinking a little bit of mead, but not that much—I may not have even gotten much of a buzz. I started to feel an odd sense of excitement coming up as the time for my performance approached, but I held back from embracing it until it was time to actually present my poem. Then came the time for my performance. My Wode-Experience began at that point, and continued through my performance. It felt like a strange flow coming forth, where it seemed like something other than myself was starting to take control of me for the presentation. Here, it is worth mentioning the definitions of the adjectives *óðr* and *wōd* in Old Norse and Old English, respectively:

- *óðr*: mad, frantic; furious, vehement, eager.
- *wōd*: senseless, mad, raging.

---

[11] Unlike the lore contests, the skaldic competitions continue to the present day. People volunteer to read poetry, sing songs, perform comedy routines, and so forth, usually around the main fire pit during the event.

[12] This poem is published in Westcoat, *Viking Poetry for Heathen Rites*, 37–38.

What I experienced seemed like a bizarre sort of fury. Reflecting on it, I can indeed see how the above adjectives would be an apt description if one had too much of it without any control. But channeled properly, it is an extremely useful force. My performance went well; I won first place with my entry. Later, during the Óðinsblót that night at ECT, at my cue to present *Hávamál* stanzas 138–44 in Old Norse, the same feeling rose up again, and may possibly have been more intense than earlier during the skaldic competition.

In June 2010, I had realized that Óðrœrir was absolutely real, on mental and spiritual levels. But here at ECT, on August 26, 2011, I experienced the reality of the Mead directly, on emotional and visceral levels. And during the reciting of poetry, no less.

Did I Hear a Word?

At an earlier time when I recorded much of this, I had been wondering if I should retroactively consider my spontaneous inspiration in early 2006 for naming the kindred Óðrœrir as a situation in which I Heard the Word Óðrœrir. I leaned toward thinking so, and I still do think so, but with some caveats. Though that was an important preparatory point, it did not lead to any real action or unfolding of Óðrœrir in my being at that time—if anything, it led only to more preparatory foundations being laid. But it can be said to be the point at which Óðrœrir entered my life to stay, though it would take four more years before my Rûna-Experience of it spurred me into proper action, for it was the realization that Óðrœrir was truly real that struck me with a sense of wonder and amazement and filled me with a sense of purpose. (It is this character of spurring to action that makes one a true initiate from having such an experience, and that is why it can be said that one internally becomes a Learner when one has such an experience.)

Looking back on it, there may be some mystery to be perceived in considering the threefold experience as a whole—the Hearing of Óðrœrir in 2006, the Rûna-Experience in June 2010, and the Wode-Experience in August 2011. Have I really Heard a Word and been called by Óðinn to Utter it? That can only be proven through Work—a lot of work. So far, every step of the way has been a great adventure. And then there was my Grail-Experience, something I absolutely did not expect prior to its occurrence in October 2013, and I turn to that now.

My Grail-Experience: Another Irruption of Power

Sometime around 2006, give or take, something else happened that would eventually become important for me. I had stumbled across the public guidebook of a then-defunct Initiatic Order of Knighthood called the Guild of the Grail, which had been founded in 2001, but disbanded around late 2002.[13] I found its spiritual message to be strangely inspiring and alluring. But I did not do much with it as my level of initiatory development was non-existent at that time, and it was, after all, a defunct order. I could do little more than hope its founder would return or someone else would restore the order. But the fascination stuck with me in the back of my mind. At some point, prior to 2009, though I don't know exactly when, I read a short essay by Edred Thorsson, titled "Graal-Mythos in Old English Runes?" in the book *Black Rûna*.[14] This really stuck in my head, and the Grail Runes have been an extremely strong interest of mine since then. Though it would be a long time before I fully realized the importance of the symbol, my fascination with Óðrœrir and the Grail Runes would lead me to creating, in September 2009, an interlocked, triple-horn logo, where each of the horns in turn were labeled with the Grail Runes: Calc, Stān, and Gār. I would first use this as the logo of my Óðrœrir Kindred (which at that time changed its name to Wodhrera Cynræden, on account of my fascination with Old English). I would eventually realize that this logo's true purpose was as a profoundly personal esoteric symbol of myself, rather than as a corporate symbol, and I would dust it off for use in my books *Eagle's Mead* and *Galdored Runes*, which are

---

[13] That public guidebook, *Liber Ars Collegium*, might still be findable on the internet somewhere.

[14] That book is out of print, but a revised and expanded version of the essay is found in Edred, *ALU*, 205–08.

filled with personal esoteric poetry.[15] However, that would take nearly 10 years. But returning to the story at hand, at this point in 2009, I was an Associate in the Rune-Gild, and would become Initiated as a Learner (1°) in November 2011. Around that time, I started thinking about my prospective Fellowship Work for the Rune-Gild, and my original idea was to create poetic stanzas for Cweorð, Calc, Stān, and Gār, in both Old English and Modern English, since these four runes do not have any surviving ancient rune poem stanzas for them. After all, in my view of things, a rune-stave isn't truly a proper rune-stave unless it has its own name and its own rune poem stanza. That three of those four were the Grail Runes was a big pull for the project.

But the time was perhaps not quite right. In August 2012, I would have a talk with my Gild-Master, Ristandi, about the project, for which I had not started writing anything. He considered it a good one, but pointed out to me that my work with researching the uses of the *galdralag* poetic meter in the Old Norse literature was already a good way toward being a Fellowship Work. I had a first draft of an academic article, and all it would need was a good additional write-up on practical applications for modern heathens. This immediately channelled all the fire in me toward such a write-up, and in short order, I completed and submitted my Fellowship Work, "Magic Metrics, Mighty Poetry: What Goals had Galdralag? What Good is Galdralag?"[16] Following this, I was named a Fellow (2°) of the Rune-Gild in February 2013. At this point, there was nothing else to draw my attention away from the Grail Runes project, and so I returned to it.

---

[15] It is on the half-title page right inside the cover in Westcoat, *Eagle's Mead*, i; for Westcoat, *Galdored Runes*, it is on the front cover.

[16] This has been published in two pieces. The academic part is Westcoat, "The Goals of *Galdralag*: Identifying the Historical Instances and Uses of the Metre," which is published academically, and the practical esoteric part is "The Good of *Galdralag*: An Inspired Look into Modern Uses for the Meter," which is in Westcoat, *Eagle's Mead*, 234–48.

In early October 2013, I completed the first full version of it, and this caused my Grail-Experience.[17] I was overcome with a profound sense of duty and devotion to the Grail and the Quest for the Grail. There was a sense that, before completing the work, I could have turned back and abandoned the Grail. But I did not, and now I crossed a point of no return. I was changed by the Grail, and realized that, at least internally, I had irrevocably become a Grail Knight. I even put my name as "Sir Eirik von Westcoat" on the first version of the project. I realized I needed a formal Grail Quest, and so I turned to those documents from the defunct Guild of the Grail, and set out to follow the initiatory path laid out in its guidebook, to the point of reaching its Knighthood on its terms. This was a series of degrees, going from Page (1°) to Squire (2°) to Knight (3°). I completed this part of my Grail Quest and reached Knighthood in June 2018. My longest poem to date, "The Ascent of a Grail Knight,"[18] is my Squire Work in that Quest, and my whole book *Eagle's Mead* is my Knighthood Work in that Quest. The Guild of the Grail material remains productive for me, as may be seen from other essays in this volume. During that path to Knighthood, I was continuing my separate progress in the Rune-Gild and was named a Master (3°) in August 2016, with my Masterwork "Three Sips from the Horn."[19]

Analyzing the Triad

Now these pieces must be looked at together, and some things said about what they have in common, and what they don't. It is clear that this kind of experience can be generalized somewhat, as the phenomenon is not limited to seeking Rûna. It is the Rûna- and Grail-Experiences that have the most in common, and the Wode-Experience is notably different in some ways. I'll start here with a

---

[17] The piece is called "Runes for the Grails," and it is published in Westcoat, *Eagle's Mead*, 249–89, 178–82 (poem translation).

[18] Westcoat, *Eagle's Mead*, 115–45.

[19] That Masterwork consisted of three pieces. The largest piece has been published as Westcoat, *Viking Poetry for Heathen Rites*. The two smaller pieces will be published eventually.

comparison of the Rûna- and Grail-Experiences, which I think are ultimately the same kind of experience on some objective level. Here are the major points of comparison:

1. What the Rûna-Experiences of myself and Edred have in common, along with my Grail-Experience, is a strong element of absolutely earnest *seeking*. That is, you must be seeking something beyond your current experience or gnosis, and sincerely seeking it for some amount of time. Edred was seeking when he had his Rûna experience. I was seeking when I had my Rûna- and Grail-Experiences.

2. Regular work at the seeking appears to be quite helpful in encouraging the experience to occur. These can be daily meditative and magical exercises, as well as special occasional rituals, particularly rituals that are highly emblematic of what is being sought. For instance, the Rune-Gild has a Rûna Working. The Guild of the Grail materials have a Rite of Ascent—but I did not have that rite at the time, and prior to my Grail-Experience, I had not been making any use of the Guild of the Grail materials which I did have.

3. The experience is dependent on subjective conditioning. In a sense, we might say it is like the familiar saying about psychedelics, that their impact on the individual will be influenced by "set and setting." The nature of that conditioning depends on what you are seeking. With my Rûna-Experience, it was the context of deliberately seeking the mysteries along with my fascination with the Mead of Poetry. With my Grail-Experience, it was a deliberate seeking of the Grail.

4. Do I think a god—in this case, Óðinn—was talking to me? Not in the sense of literal speech. I did not perceive any auditory phenomena that appeared to come from outside of myself. If Óðinn was talking to me in these experiences, it was a very subtle kind of transmission, with the result that the thoughts in my head (e.g., to name the kindred Óðrœrir, to realize that Óðrœrir is absolutely real) seemed like they came from myself, such that I could never say with absolute certainty that Óðinn gave them to me. This seems a

point that can vary from person to person, given that Edred recounts hearing Rûna from a source outside of himself.
5. The experience produces a definite sense of dedication and obligation in oneself, one that is extremely profound. It really is a case of receiving a calling, mission, or vocation. I think it would be common to perceive it as a revelation—certainly my Rûna- and Grail-Experiences were that.
6. When describing it dispassionately to others, it may not sound like a big deal, or it may not even be possible for them to understand why it's so important to you.
7. It leads to further, immediate, and enthusiastic work in the pursuit of understanding, unfolding, and developing what you experienced—just as in *Hávamál* 141, "A work got a work by a work for me." Not mere contemplation, but concrete and focused action. This final point is one of the most important—although for my Rûna-Experience, this enthusiasm took a while to get up to speed.

The Wode-Experience was different. It was not about revelation, and I did not receive a calling or vocation from it. And unlike the Rûna- and Grail-Experiences, it is something that can be trained, so that one becomes more able to call it forth on demand. In a sense, it is one way of directly experiencing the Mead of Poetry. After all, the name Óðrœrir can be translated as "frenzy-stirrer." Probably it is at least somewhat like the kind of fury that the Old Norse berserkers called forth for battle rage. Definitely the sort of force that the best kraftaskalds were able to channel, when they produced magical effects from improvised poetry.[20] It is also connected to what is called the Work of the Wode-Self in the Nine Doors curriculum.[21] It is the kind of feeling that certainly should be channeled for the best poetry performances and magical workings. And as seen from my account above, ritual invocations are helpful for calling it forth.

To conclude that analysis, I can summarize the three experiences as follows:

---

[20] See my forthcoming book, Westcoat, *Conjuring the Kraftaskalds*, which is based on my PhD dissertation.

[21] Edred, *The Nine Doors of Midgard*, 161–65, 180–81.

- Wode-Experience: a sense of fury and the true power of poetry.
- Rûna-Experience: a sense of wonder and mystery.
- Grail-Experience: a sense of solemn, supremely holy duty.

If reading this essay helps the reader to have one of those experiences, then it has helped to bring more Inspiration, more Mystery, or more Spirit into the world, and that is a good thing, for the world and its individuals sorely need such experiences to re-enchant our society and enrich our lives.

Thirty-Three, New Runes, and an Initiatory Catalyst

With all that said, a final thread needs to be mentioned, one that may entail the synthesis of my three Quests, and a different sort of experience goes with it. It has to do with the number 33, and an unexpected personal fascination with it, which for much of my life was nearly at the level of background noise. My main early memory of the number being special to me occurred late in my senior year of high school in 1995. I was preparing for college, and applied to a number of different scholarships. And I received several of them. But it was one from something called "The Big 33" which stands out in my memory far more than the others, even though it was only for $1000.[22] I remember it being something about the number, and perhaps the name, that fascinated me, although eighteen-year-old me had no idea why. Later, of course, at some point, I would hear about a well-known occult 33, namely the 33 degrees of Scottish Rite Freemasonry, but I have never felt a pull to be a Freemason. And in those Guild of the Grail materials mentioned above, they describe the symbol for its 5° as containing the number 33 in its center, which did exert some fascination on me. Of course, the Guild of the Grail's use of this number probably stems from an allusion to the aforementioned Scottish Rite. It also turns out there are a number

---

[22] The Big 33 is an annual high school all-star football game based in Pennsylvania. The scholarship in question that they sponsored was a merit-based one, open to any Pennsylvania resident, regardless of whether they played football, which I did not. They have a website, but if they are still funding college scholarships, they were not mentioned there at press time.

of other possible significances to 33, many of which I did not know about before preparing this essay.[23] And in hindsight, strangely enough, my successful attempt at working through the Nine Doors curriculum started in 2010—when I was 33 years old.

But in more recent times, my runic fascination with the number 33 comes from the aforementioned Grail Runes. It turns out that the Anglo-Saxon Futhorc had 33 runes at its fullest extent, and the final three runes of the row are those Grail Runes. And in my poem "Gar (Grail Slam Part 3)," I mention the number 33, as it is the number of the Gār rune in the Anglo-Saxon Futhorc.[24] For a time, I felt I found the true significance of the number 33 for me in that runic system. After all, the Grail Runes have been good to me, and they have brought me much esoteric growth. But no—it turns out they were not my greatest 33, but rather one of its most important harbingers.

The warm-up to this supreme 33 started in May 2021, when I got the idea for the most original piece of academic runology that I will ever write (because, frankly, it would be fiendishly difficult for me to outdo it). That is my article "The Mysteries before Rune-Staves," which proposes that the rune names and order of the Elder Futhark *preceded* runic writing on account of being an oral-traditional system for codifying Germanic alliterative verse by naming the individual sounds of the Proto-Germanic language. This immediately led me to realizing that, for my own alliterative poetry revival, I would need to give names to all the distinct sounds of modern English and that this would effectively constitute a new runic system! Oddly—or perhaps in unconscious imitation of my own academic idea—at first, I focused on this as just being an oral system with names for the individual sounds, and that staves would come later, perhaps worked out by someone else. It turns out that later was March 2023, and someone else was me. At that point, I was struck with the inspiration to try stave forms for these sounds, which I had by this point realized would need to be specific to American English (as opposed to British or Australian English, for instance). That's when the full implications

---

[23] A good internet search will turn up many of these.

[24] Westcoat, *Eagle's Mead*, 207–08.

of this project dawned on me over a relatively short period of time, producing the significant revelatory experience here. This was not to be merely a guide to alliterative sounds for poetry. This was to be the American Futharch, a full-fledged runic system for poetry, writing, magic, divination, and esotericism, to stand with equal dignity alongside the other great futharks of history: the Elder Futhark, the Younger Futhark, and the Anglo-Saxon Futhorc. It combines and synthesizes my triple quests for the Mead, the Runes, and the Grails. And the number of runes in this system, complete with academic phonology support for the total?[25] You guessed it: 33.

This realization had an effect on me that is clearly on par with the Wode-, Rûna-, and Grail-Experiences, but which is quite distinct from any of them. I can only describe it as an encounter with a sense of a fated wyrd that I must fulfill, which expresses a consummation of the deepest unique purpose and meaning of my life. Yes, a sense of "this is one of the most important things I was put on this earth to do," and that it may well define my life. Certainly one of those "leave a legacy to be remembered for" things. It also brought to mind the following, which Edred has said about Runic Initiation:

> Asgard and Hel, together they constitute the fourth level of initiation. This is the long and arduous work of the Drighten/Drightning, and is called by some the Nine Gates of Hel—by others the Nine Gates of Asgard. Herein lies a Rune. This work of the Drighten is a synthesis of the unconscious and the will. The

---

[25] The basis for this is Bizzocchi, "How Many Phonemes Does the English Language Have?", although one will have to read carefully, as the exact number 33 does not actually appear in the article. It comes from the sum of the 24 consonant phonemes and the 9 vowel phonemes of American English that he argues for, but note that I am not using his designation of semi-vowels. (Note that for the Received Pronunciation of British English, the number of phonemes is instead 35.) Though the number is 33, the same as the number of Anglo-Saxon Futhorc runes, this is actually a coincidence on the physical plane. I will not speculate here to what extent this may be a synchronicity or a deliberate arrangement on higher planes.

catalyst for the Working of this synthesis can only be provided by the god (Wōðanaz) in a personal and individual way.[26]

Have I indeed received the catalyst for that synthesis in my vision of the American Futharch? Only time will tell for sure. But if the American Futharch does not provide sufficient propulsion for my Ascent to that fourth level of Drighten (4°), I must suspect that nothing will in this lifetime. Regardless, this is truly my best and greatest 33, of that I am quite certain. Perhaps later in life I will reckon myself to have reached the 5° in the Guild of the Grail degree system and start wearing that symbol with a 33 in the center. It would be a nice thought to join Scottish Rite Freemasonry and eventually receive the 33° there, although unlikely since that kind of commitment would take too much time from expounding my own 33. But ultimately, recognition to various degrees is really only icing on the supreme 33 cake of the American Futharch itself. And beyond that, it really is about bringing my Poetic Quest and the American Futharch to a heathen world that needs them. But even if the whole world were to ignore them, I would still do this anyway. At the heart of it, the American Futharch is simply too beautiful to do otherwise.

Conclusion

This essay has essentially been a brief summary of certain significant points of my initiatory development, namely the spontaneous occurrences of certain flashes of insight and influxes of the Mead of Poetry. In a way, it's a highlight reel. It should be emphasized that there was a lot of work going on behind the scenes, only some of which was hinted at. My Fellowship Work, my Squire Work, and "Runes for the Grails" were a notable amount of writing. My Rune-Gild Masterwork and my Guild of the Grail Knighthood Work were even more writing. And there has been a lot of meditative and esoteric work, including the complete Nine Doors curriculum. If there's another take-home lesson in this, it's that the esoteric path can be an extremely long and strange one. It has been almost twenty years since Óðrœrir entered my life. It has not yet reached its full flowering in me, and

---

[26] Edred, "Initiatory Theory of the Rune-Gild," 12.

yet it has taken me many places I would never have expected to go. But I have finally crossed the threshold into truly revolutionary and immensely exciting work with it.

Works Cited

Big 33. <big33.org>.

Bizzocchi, Aldo Luiz. "How Many Phonemes Does the English Language Have?" *International Journal on Studies in English Language and Literature* (IJSELL) 5, no. 10 (October 2017): 36–46.

Edred Thorsson. *History of the Rune-Gild: The Reawakening of the Gild 1980–2018*. North Augusta, SC: Arcana Europa, 2019.

Edred Thorsson. "Initiatory Theory of the Rune-Gild." In *Mainstays from Rune-Kevels*, 12–74. Smithville, TX: The Rune-Gild, 2006.

Edred Thorsson. *The Nine Doors of Midgard: A Curriculum of Rune-Work*. 5th ed. Moss Beach, CA: The Rune-Gild, 2016.

Edred Thorsson. "*Rúnarreynsla*: The Runa-Experience and Its Role in Rune-Work." In *Mainstays from Rune-Kevels*, 73–74. Smithville, TX: The Rune-Gild, 2006. Print.

Edred Thorsson. "*Rúnarreynsla*: The Runa-Experience and Its Role in Esoteric Work." *Seek the Mysteries*. 2023. Online blog. <stephenedredflowers.substack.com/p/runarreynsla>.

Westcoat, Eirik. *Conjuring the Kraftaskalds: Magical Poets in Modern Icelandic Folklore*. Forthcoming.

Westcoat, Eirik. *Eagle's Mead: Initiatory Poetry and Prose*. Long Branch, PA: Skaldic Eagle Press, 2019.

Westcoat, Eirik. *Galdored Runes: A Portion of Eagle's Mead*. Long Branch, PA: Skaldic Eagle Press, 2020.

Westcoat, Eirik. *American Futharch*. <americanfutharch.com>.

Westcoat, Eirik. "The Goals of *Galdralag*: Identifying the Historical Instances and Uses of the Metre." *Saga-Book* 40 (2016): 69–90.

Westcoat, Eirik. "The Mysteries before Rune-Staves: Explaining Futhark Order and Rune Names via an Ur-Poem Prior to Runic Writing." Forthcoming.

Westcoat, Eirik. *Viking Poetry for Heathen Rites: Asatru Liturgy in Traditional Verse*. Long Branch, PA: Skaldic Eagle Press, 2017.

Wewelsburg's So-Called "Black Sun" is Really Himmler's Round Table and Grail

Introducing the Infamous Wewelsburg Sun Wheel

One of the most enduring mysteries of the Third Reich—and surely the most *iconic* one—is the identity of a large sun wheel design in the floor of the North Tower of Wewelsburg Castle in Germany:[1]

The Wewelsburg Sun Wheel
at the Center of the Mystery and the Controversy

For over 40 years from the end of WWII, it was all but completely ignored, but then suddenly became popularized in the early 1990s as a "black sun," largely through the novel *Die Schwarze Sonne von Tashi Lhunpo* (The Black Sun of Tashi Lhunpo), published in 1991.[2] In this entry in the occult-Nazi thriller genre, the symbol is called a black sun there, and it's used as a mark branded on the assassination victims of a cult.

From that point in time, various crowds of people have latched onto the symbol under the moniker of the "Black Sun." It seems the neo-nazi fanbois will latch onto anything "edgy"

---

[1] Photo by hwo/Alamy. It strongly accentuates the green of the marble, much more so than most other photos of the sun wheel.

[2] McCloud, *Die Schwarze Sonne*.

associated with the Third Reich, and many of them have latched onto this as a kind of substitute swastika (for use where the swastika is formally banned or otherwise unacceptable, for instance), among other things. And in response, the antifa and intelligentsia have latched onto it by demonizing it. It's a rather ridiculous game to watch, especially for a symbol that never adorned Nazi flags, did not march with their armies, and was certainly never meant as a substitute swastika. So it is needful to get to the bottom of this mysterious symbol, even if it will not change the fanatics' views about it. It is a symbol which, as we shall see, has its best explanation in something that had nothing to do with Nazi ideology at all. On the other hand, various individuals and groups of occult or neopagan orientation work with the symbol in non-nazi uses, and they are probably the ones that will be most delighted with what I say about the symbol in this essay.

But as for the "Black Sun" designation, it is thoroughly an invention of the 1990s, with no connection to the SS. For instance, a former SS folklorist at the castle, Bernhard Frank (1913–2011), had this to say about the designation:

> To my knowledge the designation Black Sun was first used after the war. I would like to say in conclusion that I never heard the term Black Sun during peacetime, that is, during my scholarly activity at Wewelsburg Castle, and also not during my wartime leaves. Is the label perhaps an invention—a malicious one I might suggest—of the post-war period?[3]

Malicious or not, "Black Sun" is very much wrong. Recent scholarship summarizes the state of knowledge about the actual meaning or name of the symbol as follows:

> All interpretations have one thing in common: They stem exclusively from the recent past and have been applied retrospectively to the sun wheel. There are no known sources from the National Socialist period that provide information about the meaning of the symbol intended at that time or about its name.[4]

---

[3] Siepe, "The Sun Wheel," 144, 156n2. Frank is quoted from an interview by Eva Kingsepp.

[4] Siepe, "The Sun Wheel," 144.

And yet there does not appear to be any genuinely plausible and complete explanations given for the symbol, whether by scholars or anyone else, after all this time. The neo-nazi fanbois go off on flights of fancy, while the credible scholars just throw up their hands and offer nothing to fill the void. Here, I will do neither—instead, I offer a complete and eminently plausible explanation that solves this mystery at last.

To be clear, I have not uncovered any never-before-seen SS documentation regarding the symbol. I'm aware that for some readers, only such documentation could ever settle the mystery. So yes, this essay is speculative, but the reader will see that all my speculations are quite reasonable. There are no flights of fancy here into bizarre Nazi occultism theories about Atlantean technology or white-supremacist Aryan-power rituals. And yet I account for *all* of the distinctive features of the symbol, including what it's doing on the castle floor—it had a real, *practical* value in Himmler's grand ambitions. My explanation here ought to become the most widely accepted explanation in the absence of SS documentation. And if such SS documentation ever turns up (though it probably won't), I'm confident that it would substantiate all of my argument here.

An Impossible Nut to Crack?

That's a bold claim to make. Many people have been fascinated by that symbol, and even a most august occultist such as Michael Aquino seemed to think the symbol was meaningless:

> The design on the floor does not seem to be anything more than an artistic abstract design which . . . went on to give rise to all sorts of crazy "explanations."[5]

The design is not abstract. It is iconic and exceptionally meaningful, with an explanation that is certainly not crazy. But I'm not so sure there's been much in the way of actual explanations so far, crazy or otherwise. Even an entire recent academic book like *Myths of Wewelsburg Castle* ultimately can't say anything about what the symbol really is. And despite it being so thick that you

---

[5] Siepe, "Esoteric Perspectives," 241n83.

could call it a "big purple brick," Pontolillo's *The Black Sun Unveiled* tells us a lot about black suns through myth and history, but it gets us no closer to deciding whether that symbol was *really* meant to be a "black sun" or something else. (Spoiler: it wasn't a black sun. And Pontolillo's book cover does not even get the proportions of the central part of the design correct.) Rather, as I will argue, the symbol has a very particular meaning, one that is noble and lofty enough for Himmler to use it to decorate the floor of the SS's Holy of Holies. The questions that I will offer answers to in this essay include:

- What does the symbol *really* depict?
- What sources is the symbol based on?
- Why does it resemble the Zierscheibe finds?
- Why did Himmler put it on the North Tower floor?

As mentioned, all of my answers to these will be eminently plausible. Nothing will be any sort of overreach. Indeed, a number of the pieces to this puzzle have been out there for a time, while others were waiting to be uncovered in the course of my research. From my title, you can see that I'm going to connect it to the Arthurian Mythos, and various idle chatter on the internet has occasionally touched on isolated elements of the correct explanation. But nobody has gone the distance before on the Arthurian hypothesis in the way I do now.

Describing the Wewelsburg Symbol

With all the controversy surrounding this symbol, it'll be good to be very exacting about it. So I start here with a precise description of the symbol. For as much as this symbol has become infamous, a discussion of this type doesn't seem to have been properly done before. As is frequently noted, its color is not black, but rather a dark, mottled green marble on an off-white marble floor. The symbol has a solid, *central circle*. But this central circle is rather peculiar, as seen in this image:[6]

---

[6] Crop and closeup of the preceding photo by hwo/Alamy.

HIMMLER'S ROUND TABLE

A Close-Up of the Sun Wheel,
Showing a Distinctive "Double" Central Circle and Core

Most of the design clearly looks like it was cut from the same batch of marble, but in the very middle of the central circle, there is a *core* with a noticeably different appearance from the rest of the marble. Pontolillo says the following about the central circle and core:

> At its very center is a shallow circular depression which, according to oral tradition, originally held a golden disk marking both the tower's central axis and the new world axis subsumed under the SS identification of the castle as the "Mid-point of the World." The fate of this disk is unknown; it was most likely removed for safe-keeping in Fall 1944 along with other castle valuables and subsequently lost.[7]

By measuring pixels in high-quality photos of this symbol, I can see that the diameter of the core looks to be slightly more than twice the width of one of the sun-wheel spokes. From various recent inquiries I've made, all indications are that there is currently

---

[7] Pontolillo, *The Black Sun Unveiled*, 44. He cites Hüser, *Wewelsburg*, 57 for this.

not a shallow depression at that core. And all the photos I've seen support that. But I've found no clear explanation of what might be going on with it, whether from the Kreismuseum Wewelsburg or anyone else. Starting from the recognition that the current core appears level with the rest of the floor, some consideration of the possibilities is needful here, since this core is significant to my argument:

1. Possibility One: The current core is original to the design, from the early 1940s, but I think this unlikely. If that is the case, it confirms that the core was indeed meant to be distinctive in some fashion. The central circle is made of six triangular wedges, and though you can see the seams between them, they don't clash with each other, and look nice as a whole. But the core does clash and stands out. Had Himmler and company wanted it to blend in with the rest of the central circle, it would have been easy to make it from the same batch of marble as the central circle and rest of the sun wheel. But given how drab the core is compared to the rest, it strongly suggests that it was a placeholder for something more impressive. In this scenario, the legendary gold disk is as good a possibility as any, and undoubtedly yet another grandiose idea of Himmler's that never got implemented.
2. Possibility Two: There was a depression and perhaps a gold disk as indicated, but it was filled in with the current core late in the war or in the postwar period. If that is the case, perhaps a more closely matching marble or something else is underneath it. Filling it in later would easily explain why it's not the same batch of marble, namely that there wasn't any leftover to use. An eventual fill-in during the postwar period would actually be quite sensible. Any depression left to remain would be an injury or damage hazard, given enough foot traffic, not to mention a bit unsightly, especially if it was deep enough. Ultimately, this possibility also confirms the core as deliberately distinctive, even if we cannot see what was once there.

This sufficiently covers the two possibilities for the current core (original vs. not original), and in the end, the inescapable conclusion is that the core was meant by Himmler to be different and distinctive in some fashion (even if we cannot decide among the possibilities), and thus it's a design element that requires an explanation. The legend of the gold disk is as good a place as any to start, especially since I will suggest a source for it. And that source is not a mere "one-off" or an attempt to awkwardly shoehorn the gold disk in, but rather a source that contributes a total of *three* elements to the sun wheel's design that *all* fit perfectly into the whole. But now it's time to consider the rest of the symbol.

Right outside of the solid central circle, there is a very close *inner ring* (also seen in the close-up just above). The thickness of the ring appears roughly the same as that of the sun-rune spokes. The distance between the central circle and the inner ring is roughly one-half the thickness of the sun-rune spokes, making this a very close-fitting inner ring. At a comfortable distance, there is an *outer ring* (visible in the photo that opens this essay). Equally placed along the outer ring are the twelve *sun-rune spokes*. Each spoke spans from the outer ring to the central circle, crossing the inner ring as it goes. These sun-rune spokes are "reversed"—that is, they are in the opposite direction from the typical Sól rune (Younger Futhark) or Sig rune (Armanen Futharkh) that they appear to be modeled on (more on that later). And finally, the "arms" of these sun-rune spokes are *very noticeably* unequal in length. That is, each goes a short distance from the outer ring, then makes its horizontal "zag" before then running a much longer distance to reach the inner ring and the central circle.

How big is this symbol on the floor? Apparently, this information is not generally available, nor have writers on the symbol included such details, which is a deficiency. Comparing a number of pictures that show the room with furniture or people near or on top of parts of the symbol,[8] I give it an estimate of about four meters in diameter. Again, by counting pixels in photos, the diameter of the *core* appears to be about seven percent of the whole symbol's diameter, or roughly 28 centimeters. An 18–24 karat gold plate of that size would be magnificently impressive.

---

[8] Such as John-Stucke and Siepe, *Myths of Wewelsburg Castle*, ix.

Looking at the rest of the room, the marble inlays accentuate the concentric nature of the design. That is, the off-white or off-gray marble of the rest of the room is effectively in concentric rings around the symbol.

Let it be noted that I consider the unequal arms of the sun-rune spokes—and the peculiar core, central circle, and inner ring combination—to be *extremely important* in interpreting this symbol, and I find it quite shocking that these attributes seem to have been downright ignored by prior commentators. But for now, let's move on to its context in the Wewelsburg North Tower.

The Wewelsburg North Tower

The symbol's sole original surviving existence anywhere is in the form of the above floor mosaic decoration in the North Tower of Wewelsburg Castle near Paderborn, Westphalia, in Germany. This main, ground-level floor of the North Tower is known as the *Obergruppenführersaal* (Senior Group Leaders Hall).[9] Henceforth, I will call it the OGF Hall, to avoid tormenting the reader by repeating this long, awkward German word. But it's worth mentioning what an *Obergruppenführer* (senior group leader) was for the SS. During most of the Third Reich, this was the second-highest rank in the SS, after only the *Reichsführer-SS* (Reich Leader of the SS). *Reichsführer-SS* was the head of the order, and this was Heinrich Himmler from 1929 to 1945, covering the entire relevant time period in this article. Only in 1942 was the rank of *Oberst-Gruppenführer* (highest group leader, Oberst-GF) created above the regular OGF, and only four people ever held it. Contrasting that, about 100 men had the rank of OGF by the end of the war. The OGF Hall, judging by its name, was meant to have special importance and function for these men.

The OGF Hall is very striking and well-lit. Twelve light-green sandstone columns and arches go around this circular hall, and there are many windows. Most of the floor is a whitish-gray

---

[9] The names of the various North Tower rooms are securely attested, but they are in sources that are not easy for a layperson to access. See John-Stucke, "Himmler's Plans," 30n82.

marble, with the sun wheel standing out for its mottled dark green. Here is a picture of the hall with the sun wheel visible:[10]

The OGF Hall in Wewelsburg today

Rüdiger Sünner notes that the OGF Hall bears a striking resemblance to the Grail Hall as depicted in the 1882 debut of Wagner's opera *Parsifal* in the Bayreuth Festspielhaus. Sünner goes a bit further with his observations and refers to the sun wheel, saying:

> Die Kreisform von Saal und Bodenornament lassen durchaus Assoziationen zum Begriff »Tafelrunde« zu.
>
> The circular shape of the hall and the floor ornament certainly suggest associations with the term "Round Table."[11]

He came remarkably close to the target here. But he did not pursue it further, and that is the only time he mentions the Round

---

[10] "Obergruppenführersaal mit Schwarzer Sonne, Wewelsburg," *Wikimedia Commons*. Photo by Dirk Vorderstraße. The castle currently houses both a museum and a youth hostel. The OGF hall isn't part of the hostel, but the bean bags seem to be a nod to it in an attempt to "neutralize" the allure of the hall.

[11] Sünner, *Schwarze Sonne*, 133, 146–47. Translation mine.

Table in the book, and he goes off in a different direction about the possible symbolism of the number 12 after that statement. Several others have concurred regarding the resemblance to the *Parsifal* Grail Hail, and Sünner isn't necessarily the first. Michael Aquino took this view also—"What I call the 'Grail Hall' above the Gruft is an enlightening, ennobling, environment: very much Parsifal's Grail Castle"—and Siepe mentions others who have discussed the *Parsifal* resemblance.[12] But none went on to explain why the OGF Hall should look like that Grail Hall. Here is a circa-1882 rendering of that Wagnerian Grail Hall in *Parsifal*:[13]

Act III stage design of *Parsifal* by Paul von Joukowsky (1845–1912)

One can see the Grail being held up quite prominently in the center of the room. If the OGF Hall was intended to look like this, might it also have a Grail? I will return to that question later.

---

[12] Siepe, "Esoteric Perspectives," 219–20, 242n92; Siepe, "The 'Grail Castle' of the SS," 67, 89.

[13] "Parsifal 1882 Act 3," *Wikimedia Commons*.

Let us look at the rest of the tower for now. Below the OGF Hall is a room known as *Die Gruft* (The Crypt), which I will simply call the Gruft, as that is common in many sources. The room used to be a cistern, but the SS renovations lowered the floor significantly. Here is a picture of the Gruft showing both the ceiling and floor:[14]

The Gruft with a strange swastika on the ceiling
and the central depression in the floor.

There is a broad, central depression in the room. A pipe was installed in the center. Most commentators have interpreted this as a gas pipe for an eternal flame in the center. (But I will consider an

---

[14] Photo by hwo/Alamy.

alternate possibility in a moment.) The acoustics of the room have powerful reverberations for anyone standing in that central depression, leading to the conclusion that this was meant for rituals of some kind.[15] Twelve pedestals are around the edge of the room, each of which reportedly had a wall niche above it. The domed ceiling has a significant swastika decoration in the middle of it, as seen in the picture above. But it is misleading to just call it a swastika, as it is not an ordinary swastika. Rather, it is a typical four-armed swastika with plenty of extra "dangly bits" coming off each arm. The Nazis loved swastikas, and the SS could have easily made this a mere ordinary one, but they did not. A satisfactory explanation of this swastika must account for those extra bits and the context of this room. The YouTube channel Beyond Room 313 made one that I agree with. He interprets the swastika symbol as the roots of a tree, namely the World Tree, so that the Gruft is a chamber beneath the World Trees's roots.[16] That's all good so far. Correspondingly, he thinks the pipe was for water, not fire, making a small pool that would be a kind of Mímir's Well. He further goes on to see the sun wheel in the OGF Hall as a depiction of the World Tree itself. These other parts I don't necessarily agree with. I'm not taking a position on what that pipe was for. And I think the whole North Tower was meant to be the World Tree, not the relatively small sun wheel in the OGF Hall. A World Tree explanation for the sun wheel symbol may sound nice, but it cannot account for all of the distinctive features of the symbol.

What is clear from all of this is that the OGF Hall and Gruft, with their stunning designs, were meant to make a profound impression on those who visited them. That's a key part of them being cult and ritual sites. But when did these stunning rooms reach their current form, with the magnificent sun wheel on the floor? They were not always like that.

When Himmler took possession of the castle, the North Tower was a burned-out shell and not much fit for use. It would

---

[15] Both Sünner and Aquino have noted this, see Siepe, "The 'Grail Castle' of the SS," 67; Siepe, "Esoteric Perspectives," 214–15.

[16] Beyond Room 313, "Wewelsburg Without the Nonsense."

be some time before Himmler's dream of a Center of the World would begin to unfold, but ultimately it did. But first, in 1935, a blacksmith's shop was put in the North Tower to produce decorations and furnishings for the castle.[17] This, to my mind, is an adequate indication that the Tower had not yet been given the sacred character it was ultimately meant to have, and so the sun wheel was surely not on the floor there yet.[18] The Tower started taking shape in 1939 with plans from Hermann Bartels (Himmler's architect for all things Wewelsburg) that turned the basement cistern into the Gruft and that blacksmith's shop into the majestic OGF Hall. Exactly when this occurred is unclear, but these renovations did take place, starting in 1941–1942.[19] It is most likely during this time that the infamous sun wheel was installed in the floor of the OGF Hall. In April 1944, all renovations were halted with the tower unfinished, but the OGF Hall and Gruft were somewhat completed.[20] This was not the limit of Himmler's vision, and I will touch on the further plans later.

The Wewelsburg Castle Itself

Now I turn to the history of the castle itself during the Third Reich. I won't go into its further past, except to say that it was built in its more-or-less current form in the early 1600s. After a visit to the castle in 1933, Himmler decided to acquire it for the SS, and in 1934, he secured it from the local district authority. What was this castle for? It was to be an SS leadership school, concerned with ideological instruction of SS leaders. The formal takeover by the SS occurred in September 1934, and the *Völkischer*

---

[17] John-Stucke, "Himmler's Plans," 9–10.

[18] Pontolillo, *The Black Sun Unveiled*, 44 points out that a 1922 photo of a different part of the floor of the North Tower shows a completely different stone cladding than what is seen today, giving another indication that the sun wheel was not yet there.

[19] John-Stucke, "Himmler's Plans," 16–19 and figure 1.11. Pontolillo, *The Black Sun Unveiled*, 37, concurs.

[20] Pontolillo, *The Black Sun Unveiled*, 40.

Beobachter (the newspaper of the NSDAP) reported on it with much fanfare. I quote them here, for their words capture the spirit of the matter quite well:

> Mit dem heutigen Tage ist die alte, trutzige Feste Wewelsburg, an historischer Stätte im alten Sachsenlande gelegen, von der S.S. der N.S.D.A.P. in ihre Obhut übernommen worden, um als Reichsführerschule der S.S. künftighin zu dienen. Damit hat die Wewelsburg, die auf eine lange und ruhmvolle Bedeutung in der deutschen Geschichte zurückblicken kann, auch im Dritten Reich einen Platz von historischer Bedeutung zugewiesen erhalten. Denn hier sollen jene Männer weltanschaulich, gesinnungsmäßig und körperlich geschult werden, die berufen sind, in der S.S. ein Führeramt zu bekleiden, die als Vorbild und Führer vor dem Kern gesunder deutscher Jugend herziehen sollen. . . . Bei ihrem Wirken an dieser historischen Stätte würden sich die hier zu schulenden Führer der S.S. bewusst werden, welche Verantwortung sie vor der deutschen Geschichte zu übernehmen hätten.
>
> As of today, the old, defiant Wewelsburg fortress, located at a historic site in the old Saxon region, has been taken over by the SS of the NSDAP to serve as the Reich Leadership School of the SS in the future. Thus, Wewelsburg, which can look back on a long and glorious significance in German history, has also been assigned a place of historical significance in the Third Reich. For here, those men are to be trained ideologically, morally, and physically who are called upon to hold a leadership position in the SS, who are to act as role models and leaders before the core of healthy German youth. . . . Through their work at this historic site, the SS leaders being trained here would become aware of the responsibility they bore before German history.[21]

Put more simply, the castle is meant to help cultivate a warrior elite to lead the SS. We will see more evidence in that direction as we go on, and I offer my view on how heavy that responsibility before German history was ultimately meant to be. But why this site in the Paderborn district? I won't enter into that here. There

---

[21] John-Stucke, "22. September 1934," *Internet-Portal „Westfälische Geschichte"* which is quoting from *Völkischer Beobachter*, September 27, 1934 (Ausgabe A, No. 270). Translation mine.

are fanciful theories out there, ranging from supposed ancient prophecies (The Battle of the Birch Tree) and geomantic energy centers or ley lines. I'm not passing judgment on them one way or another; they are simply irrelevant to my argument about the Wewelsburg sun wheel. It is clear enough that the site was meant as a "Center of the World" location for the SS, regardless of why the site itself was chosen for that purpose. Though it should be noted that the early actual uses of the castle did not get around to the high-minded leadership school Himmler envisioned, the later plans and renovations adequately show that he never abandoned his dream of cultivating a warrior elite at this site.

And Himmler indeed got started on bringing his warrior elite to the site and gradually closing it to outsiders. In November 1935, he put a ban on visitations to the site. In May 1938, Himmler and nine high-ranking SS officers had a meeting at the castle.[22] Then, later that year, "Himmler announced that he intended in future to hold a conference of Gruppenführer every spring at the Wewelsburg, and to use the occasion to swear in the new Gruppenführer."[23] Not long after, in 1939, he decided the site should be further kept out of the prying eyes of the public by suppressing publications about it. In June 1941, he held a meeting at the castle with senior SS leaders to prepare them mentally for Operation Barbarossa and the planned extermination of 30 million people in the Soviet Union, although the North Tower was still under construction.[24] It shows that though Himmler had grand, high-minded plans for the castle, he apparently didn't see their deep contradiction with industrial-scale mass murder.[25]

---

[22] John-Stucke, "Himmler's Plans," 15.

[23] Longerich, *Heinrich Himmler*, 295.

[24] Longerich, *Heinrich Himmler*, 522–23; John-Stucke, "Himmler's Plans," 23–24.

[25] Himmler's additional monstrosities relating to concentration camps, exterminations, and mass murder are well documented. One may see, for instance, any of the chapters of part 5 found in Longerich, *Heinrich Himmler*, 515–643. I touch on only the planned Russian extermination in my main text, as that was something that he specifically used Wewelsburg in connection with.

Occult Mead

Ultimately, the castle was to be limited to the SS Gruppenführer (and higher ranks) and various high-level guests.[26]

A concern with history, myth, and ideology is clear from the names given to the various rooms of the castle. The names survive from three different sources, of which there is some overlap.[27] But merging them gives the following, and in categories of my designation:

- *Kings*: King Arthur, King Henry, Frederick the Great.
- *Other People*: Reichsführer room, Mad Christian (that is, Christian of Brunswick), Christopher Columbus, Henry the Lion, Widukind.
- *Organizations*: Teutonic Knights, Vehmic Court.
- *Locations*: Westphalia, Marienburg.
- *Ideas*: New Nobility, Blood and Soil, Race Issues.
- *Other*: Grail, Aryan, Seasons and Runes, German Language.

It is quite a mixed bag, but in particular, King Arthur, Grail, New Nobility, Teutonic Knights, Marienburg (a prior capital of the Teutonic Knights) show the concerns with historical and legendary exemplars of knighthood. Today, the Knights Templar are a more familiar name to most readers. But the Teutonic Knights were one of the other great knightly orders of the Middle Ages, and it should surprise no one that the SS would pick the German order to focus on.

Having noted only two rooms that directly touch on Arthurian matters, here is a good place to address a particular objection from the academic literature:

> Wewelsburg Castle seems to be known to a broader public primarily as an SS "Grail castle" and "cult site." This is astonishing on closer inspection, for there is simply no evidence that Grail mythology played a large, let alone paramount role in the SS's development of Wewelsburg Castle. The legend's influence is only evident in the naming of two of the castle's rooms that bore the names *King Arthur* and *Grail*. The latter contained a thematically fitting piece of quartz or rock crystal, and its furnishing, as with some other rooms, was a topic of dispute between the castle

---

[26] John-Stucke, "Himmler's Plans," 16.

[27] John-Stucke, "Himmler's Plans," 10–11.

administrator and the architect. However, the rooms with Arthurian associations were only two among many, with the others bearing names with quite different thematic origins.[28]

I am not arguing that the Grail mythology played a *large* role in the development of the castle *as a whole*, and I'm certainly not disputing the variety of thematic origins for the room names. But I feel Siepe (and likely others) were, quite wrongly, expecting that Himmler would have been more thematically consistent if he were intending Wewelsburg to be a "Grail Castle" in some sense. There's no thematic consistency anywhere to be found in the castle, whether for Arthurian themes or anything else. For instance, the above-mentioned Gruft has no identifiable Arthurian themes whatsoever as far as I can tell (nor is there any for what we know of the plans for the Gruppenführer Hall, which I mention in the next section below). It seems a case of if looks German, it fits.[29] I think Himmler may have taken the *general idea* of making Wewelsburg into an SS spiritual headquarters (a Grail Castle in that sense) from the portrayal of Munsalvæsche in Wolfram's *Parzival*. But that is all, and not the same as thinking he would necessarily drill down to use all of the fine details in decorating Wewelsburg to constantly remind everyone it was the new Munsalvæsche. Himmler would probably have thought such consistency too limiting to his free artistry in such matters. And we would look in vain to find evidence that Himmler's use of any mythological themes for his purposes (propaganda or otherwise) was ever consistent. Longerich's chapter, "Ideology and Religious Cult," makes Himmler's syncretic nature clear enough, if the reader wishes for more examples than what I mention in the course of this essay.[30]

---

[28] Siepe, "The 'Grail Castle' of the SS," 33.

[29] A room named Christopher Columbus does seem to be an outlier. Perhaps it is a nod to their Italian allies. Himmler was not against having some admiration for cultures that he viewed as worthy vis-à-vis Germany (such as the Japanese samurai, see Longerich, *Heinrich Himmler*, 281), even if we might view this as merely convenient opportunism with regard to Germany's allies leading up to the war.

[30] Longerich, *Heinrich Himmler*, 255–98.

Instead, my argument here simply entails recognizing just one more Grail-themed room in Wewelsburg, albeit one that got significantly more thought put into it on account of its location in the North Tower and the specific purpose I believe was intended for it. But the war ultimately put an end to Himmler's plans for the castle. As Allied forces closed in on Wewelsburg, the castle was abandoned. Himmler ordered the destruction of the castle, and on March 31, 1945, the attempt was made. But the SS company carrying out the operation had insufficient explosives, never planting any in the North Tower itself. So they set the castle on fire and fled. The attempted demolition was largely a failure, and the OGF Hall and Gruft appear to have been untouched, but now the castle was open to looting from nearby villagers. A few days later, on April 2, American troops secured the area.[31]

The Unrealized Future Plans for the Site

Beyond the OGF Hall and the Gruft, there were significant plans by Bartels in October 1941 for the increase of the North Tower to rebuild the floors above the OGF Hall, pictured in the blueprints below:[32]

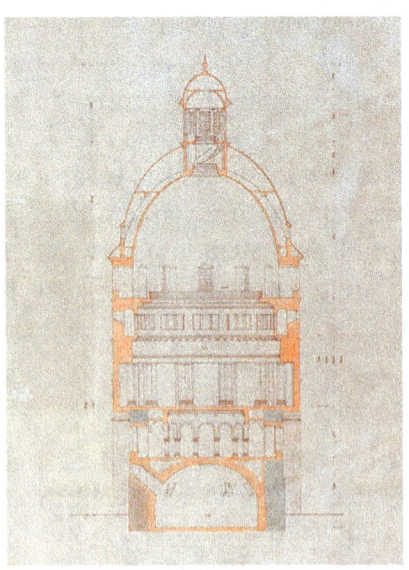

---

[31] Pontolillo, *The Black Sun Unveiled*, 38–39.

[32] John-Stucke, "Himmler's Plans," 17.

The Gruft and OGF Hall are the two small rooms on the bottom. The center of this blueprint is the Gruppenführer Hall (GF Hall—the Gruppenführer were next in rank below the OGFs), while a spacious dome and then a cupola sits at the top. The GF Hall was to "be hung with the coats-of-arms of deceased Gruppenführer and was intended to be both a future induction site as well as a general ceremonial meeting place for officers of this rank."[33] This is a ritual element to promote the honor and esprit de corps of the SS elite, another note in the symphony that included the traditions surrounding the infamous Death's Head ring of the SS. One of those traditions was that the rings of SS men who died with honor were to be kept at the castle, specifically in the Gruft.[34] Showing that Himmler's grandiose dreams truly had no limit, plans from 1944 for the future expansion of the site after the "Final Victory" would have grown it into a very large complex:[35]

---

[33] Pontolillo, *The Black Sun Unveiled*, 42. He is citing Himmler's speech before assembled Gruppenführer at Bad Tölz, 18 February 1937, as reproduced in Ackermann, *Heinrich Himmler*, 105. Many other sources, too numerous to list, instead have the distortion that the coats-of-arms of the deceased were to be burned in the Gruft.

[34] Flowers and Moynihan, *The Secret King*, 53, citing Hüser, *Wewelsburg*, 66–67.

[35] John-Stucke, "Himmler's Plans," 22, cropped slightly.

Though some sources would deny that the spearhead-like shape was intended to be a spear, it is difficult to look at it and see anything else. It even has a long, straight road as the "spear shaft." Surely Himmler and Bartels did not intend a mason's trowel! In any case, the small black triangle at the tip of the "spear" is Wewelsburg Castle, and the small black dot at the northern tip of that is the North Tower of the castle. It is immediately apparent that the entire site is planned around the North Tower, complete with concentric circular roads and other structures at varying distances, some a bit extreme. (The tower would surely appear small in the distance to someone looking at it from the outermost road!) All of it is meant to impress upon the visitors that there is something special in that North Tower, and that it is both figuratively and literally the center of the SS world at this most grandiose retreat site. Now it is time to consider the dreamer of this dream, Heinrich Himmler.

Heinrich Himmler: The Boss Man Himself

Ultimately, the most important person in figuring out what the Wewelsburg symbol means is Heinrich Himmler (1900–1945). As already mentioned, Himmler was the head of the SS and effectively answered only to Hitler. He had a relatively free hand with the running of Wewelsburg and his ambitions for its future. But where was this all going?

Himmler kept a diary and records of reading lists from his youth well into adulthood. They showed an eclectic interest in esotericism, in addition to the right-wing political ideology that is expected. Pontolillo surmises that these years of self-study led Himmler to a worldview "characterized by three main tenets: an absolute belief in God, the importance of maintaining an elite body of warriors, and the exercise of a radical utilitarianism with respect to all ideological issues."[36] The belief in God did not mean Christianity, which he was hostile to. And here, I contend that the second tenet about elite warriors was driving Himmler's plans for Wewelsburg's North Tower. Though Karl Wolff (1900–1984), Himmler's chief of staff, is not always considered a reliable witness

---

[36] Pontolillo, *The Black Sun Unveiled*, 14.

about his former boss, he did mention in a 1961 interview that although Himmler spoke "grand words full of pathos" about organizing the SS "according to the tradition of the old German knightly orders . . . [we] did not take them any more seriously than his other speeches about the need to revive Germanic ideals."[37] But there is plenty more from others to back up the general sentiments he attributed to Himmler. Pontolillo clarifies further regarding Himmler's warrior elite ideas:

> With respect to his elite Waffen-SS, the model most admired by Himmler was that of the Kshatriya caste (the warrior caste of the Hindus). He felt that such a system was Germany's pathway to salvation.[38]

Himmler himself specifically invoked the ideal of knighthood on occasion. In a talk to SS leaders, Himmler called the SS an "order of knights that no one who, by virtue of his blood, has been accepted into can ever leave; he belongs to it body and soul as long as his earthly life shall last."[39] There are probably more examples that could be turned up. Himmler's knighthood talk made an impression on Hermann Fegelein (who seems to have taken it more seriously than Wolff) when, in a letter to Himmler in October 1943, Fegelein attributed to Himmler the words "We have to do more than our duty: as knights without fear or reproach," though it is not clear when he heard that from Himmler.[40]

---

[37] Siepe, "The 'Grail Castle' of the SS," 46. I should acknowledge here that both Karl Wolff and Felix Kersten made claims in the post-war period about Himmler's fascination with the Round Table and Arthurian Mythos, but I have not made use of them. Their claims on this and many other matters are often thought to be embellished. But none of them are necessary for accepting my arguments here.

[38] Pontolillo, *The Black Sun Unveiled*, 15. Here, he is citing Longerich, *Heinrich Himmler*, 84.

[39] Longerich, *Heinrich Himmler*, 352–53, 839. From a speech at the leaders' conference of the SS-Oberabschnitt South-East in Breslau, January 19, 1935.

[40] Longerich, *Heinrich Himmler*, 306.

And what might all this invoking of knighthood be for? Even in the early days of Himmler's leadership of the SS, he had a clear idea of what he wanted the SS to become, namely Germany's finest warrior elite, for he said so in June 1931:

> The SS must become a force that includes the best human material that we still possess in Germany. . . . We are on the way to becoming a force that is better than a military unit, that is more disciplined than they are. Only when we can claim to compete with the best military unit shall we have earned the right to wear the death's-head badge. . . . The best soldiers, the best Germans will come to us of their own accord, we will not need to seek them, if they see that the SS has been set up correctly, that the SS is really good.[41]

Himmler doubtlessly had myriad approaches to cultivating that, and his racial and physical standards for SS membership are well known. But I focus here on how he was very keen to use ritual and symbolism to inspire—to *in*form—the SS elite regarding the high station he wanted them to occupy. The famous Death's Head ring will be discussed later along with Wiligut, and Himmler's ritual and ceremonial ideas for the SS were quite extensive beyond that. Selected SS leaders received special swords with the words:

> I confer on you the sword of the SS. Never draw it without need! Never sheath it without honor! Preserve your own honor as unconditionally as you are committed to respecting the honor of others and to acting chivalrously to defend the defenseless![42]

There was more. There was a special brooch for SS men to give to their wives when they became mothers, and only to be worn by such mothers. There were even detailed birth, marriage, and burial rites for SS members. Summer solstice and Yule celebrations even got his attention.[43]

---

[41] Longerich, *Heinrich Himmler*, 122–23. From a talk Himmler gave to SS leaders.

[42] Longerich, *Heinrich Himmler*, 288–92.

[43] Longerich, *Heinrich Himmler*, 288. I discuss a naming rite later with Wiligut.

He certainly didn't limit such ambitions to his SS. For a number of years, starting in 1934, Himmler also eyed the nearby Externsteine site as a kind of holy site, and in 1940, he had decided it should be a nature preserve and something to be aligned with his ideology and vision, and that "the public must be educated to behave as if in a truly sacred place."[44] Did Himmler really believe in all this? He certainly seems to have, but more importantly than that, he clearly wanted his SS elite to believe it. If the Externsteine was to be so sacred to the German public, would he not also try to make a sacred place that was exclusively for his SS elite? Wewelsburg castle, and in particular its North Tower, was clearly his choice for that. The recent academic literature recognizes Himmer's integrated strategy on such matters with this summary of approaches to Himmler and Wewelsburg:

> Wewelsburg Castle has accordingly ceased being seen as a quirk of Himmler's historical romanticism and is now viewed as a component of his efforts to establish a new tradition promoting the cohesion of the SS. The storage of the death's head rings at the castle and the gathering of coats of arms for display there served this purpose. This context also includes the SS's reference to historical role models, such as the Teutonic Knights, Henry I, and Frederick the Great, not to mention the introduction of SS's own customs. This new view of SS ideology, in contrast to the older literature, emphasizes, among other things, the organization's hostility to history and notes that ideology for Himmler was instrumental in character—even if not exclusively.[45]

I am quite in agreement with this view. From that short tour and further matters to be mentioned ahead, it's clear enough that Himmler valued ritual and symbolism as essential and instrumental tools for his project of cultivating the ultimate esprit de corps for the SS. And I will interpret the Wewelsburg sun wheel as another piece in that sprawling grand design, one that was aimed at the highest of the hierarchy that would gather at Wewelsburg for ceremonies and rituals, although the war would ensure that it did not reach the full flowering of its intended use.

---

[44] Longerich, *Heinrich Himmler*, 296–97.

[45] Siepe, "The 'Grail Castle' of the SS," 64.

Karl Maria Wiligut, Occultist on Staff

After Himmler himself, the most important figure in this mystery is Karl Maria Wiligut (1866–1946). Born to a military family, Wiligut joined the military early in life, serving in the Austro-Hungarian Army. He also had an interest in occultism from relatively early in life, joining a para-masonic lodge in 1889. He had the acquaintance of members of the Ordo Novi Templi. After serving with distinction in World War I, he retired from the army as a colonel with an excellent record in 1919, and continued his occult studies in the vicinity of Salzburg. But in the post-war years, his relationship with his wife became increasingly strained, and in late 1924, he was forcibly committed to an insane asylum for a few years. He was released in 1927, and remained in the area until 1932, when he met an influential early member of the NSDAP and Edda Society, Frieda Dorenberg. She arranged for Wiligut's move from Austria to Germany, near Munich. Soon after, a long-time friend introduced him to Heinrich Himmler. In early 1933, the National Socialists took power in Germany, and Wiligut joined the SS later that year. He was soon promoted to colonel (*SS-Standartenführer*). In 1935, he became part of Himmler's personal staff. His work was somewhat similar to that of the Ahnenerbe in regards to German heritage matters, but wholly separate from it, and he answered to Himmler personally.[46] It is clear that Himmler valued him highly. But Wiligut acquired enemies, and Himmler's chief of personal staff, Karl Wolff, discovered in November 1938 that Wiligut had spent time in an insane asylum. That controversy proved too much of a liability. Wiligut's retirement was arranged and officially dated August 28, 1939.[47] But Himmler would continue to admire Wiligut and contact him from time to time:

> Significantly, [Himmler] kept Wiligut's death's-head ring, which he had had to give back when he left the SS, in his own strongroom. And he still called on Wiligut for advice, for example

---

[46] Flowers and Moynihan, *The Secret King*, 44–49. For a longer biography, see also Goodrick-Clarke, *The Occult Roots of Nazism*, 177–91.

[47] Flowers and Moynihan, *The Secret King*, 59–60.

in the summer of 1940, when he was having an emblem designed for the graves of fallen SS men. . . . Finally, Himmler's office diary for November 1941 indicates a lunch with 'Colonel Wiligut' in Berlin.[48]

This timeline of Wiligut's SS involvement adequately allows for his participation in the design of the Wewelsburg sun wheel at the time I will argue for, though it may extend into his retirement slightly.

Now I turn to Wiligut's occultism during his time in the SS. Testifying to their strong relationship, Himmler and Wiligut corresponded frequently, and Himmler initialed and kept many of Wiligut's letters among his private papers. Most significantly for my purposes here, one of the surviving letters included a draft of Wiligut's article for *Hagal*, "Gotos Raunen—Runenwissen!"[49] This shows Himmler's exposure to Wiligut's peculiar runology and the Zil rune (to be introduced later) that will be part of my analysis.

In 1997, Manfred Lenz interviewed Gabriele Dechend, who had known Wiligut while he was alive. She reports reading Otto Rahn's book on the Grail (*The Crusade against the Grail*), and giving it to Wiligut, who made Himmler aware of it—establishing the enthusiasm of our two main principals in Grail matters. Dechend also reports arranging a meeting with Rahn at Himmler's request, and this ultimately leading to Rahn joining Himmler's staff.[50] The three—Himmler, Wiligut, and Rahn—seemed to be quite keen on Grail matters. Goodrick-Clarke notes that "in September 1935 Rahn wrote excitedly to [Wiligut] about the places he was visiting in his hunt for Grail traditions in Germany, asking complete confidence in the matter with the exception of Himmler."[51]

---

[48] Longerich, *Heinrich Himmler*, 285.

[49] Goodrick-Clarke, *The Occult Roots of Nazism*, 183–84, 259n14.

[50] Flowers and Moynihan, *The Secret King*, 181–82.

[51] Goodrick-Clarke, *The Occult Roots of Nazism*, 189, 260n36. Goodrick-Clarke is citing a letter by Rahn, dated 27 September 1935, Bundesarchiv, Koblenz, Nachlass Himmler 19.

Returning to the Lenz interview, he also asks Dechend about the Wewelsburg floor design being a "Black Sun," and implies Wiligut's connection to it. Her response touches on the number of the sun-rune spokes:

> It seems to me that a definite correlation between the "Black Sun" and the design in the [OGF Hall] is quite improbable. Only very recently have I ever heard anything about a "Black Sun." I find this to be a rather unusual theory, not to mention a foggy one. If the suggestion for the design is supposed to have come from [Wiligut], I would be more inclined to say that the "12" has to do with the zodiac and the other meanings to which the holy number corresponds.[52]

She proceeds to relate an incident in which Wiligut interpreted 12 small circles on an unusual prehistoric stone as the signs of the zodiac. Wiligut's fascination with the zodiac manifested elsewhere, too; he made the start of an esoteric synthesis of it by corresponding Norse/Germanic names and rune-staves to the 12 astrological signs.[53]

Wiligut's Naming Rite and the Death's Head Ring

There is a record of a SS name-giving rite conducted by Wiligut in the presence of Himmler in January 1937 for the son of SS-Brigadier General Karl Wolff, who had been born a few weeks prior. The child's mother, SS-Major General R. Heydrich, and SS-Captain Karl Diebitsch were also present. The tokens involved in the rite included a blue ribbon, a cup, a spoon, and a ring. The rite notes that the "child will be entered into the birth-registry of the SS and noted down in the clan-book of the SS."[54] Though the rite calls upon "Got" as the source of all life, it is clearly not a Christian-inspired rite, and one suspects Wiligut used his own peculiar understanding of Got. German identity is invoked several times, with the clear implication that the boy should grow up to reflect well on the German nation. Nominally, such a rite is for the

---

[52] Flowers and Moynihan, *The Secret King*, 183–84.

[53] Flowers and Moynihan, *The Secret King*, 112–14.

[54] Flowers and Moynihan, *The Secret King*, 158–60.

child, but in actuality, it is much more so for the mother and especially the SS father of the child, to impress upon them their duty to bring up the child in a manner befitting an officer of the SS. It is unclear how widely this rite was meant to be deployed, but the attendees list confirms that high-ranking officers were among the intended audience.

Wiligut is also credited with the design of the infamous Death's Head Ring (*Totenkopfring*). When an SS-man received the ring, it came with an accompanying text explaining its symbols.[55] These straightforwardly discuss loyalty to the *Führer*, a preparedness to sacrifice oneself for the good of the collective, reconnecting with their past, identity as a member of the SS, victory, and Germany. The ring, of course, seems quite syncretic. For instance, one imagines the Death's Head was a medieval *memento mori* inclusion, though it strikes me as a bit out-of-place next to runes and oak leaves. Nevertheless, the whole is iconically powerful and still commands fascination 80 years later. For Himmler, whose name appears on the explanatory text, the ring was clearly one of his ceremonial tools for molding the SS into a warrior elite. The rings were widespread enough, for they went to the first 2000 members of the SS, and the leaders after they had been members for some years.[56]

Surely Himmler did not neglect planning such ceremonies and ritual tools for the very top of the hierarchy, the OGFs. We simply didn't get any surviving documents on what he was thinking of. We have only the OGF Hall and its strange sun wheel —in a way, it is like any mysterious archaeological find, like a peculiar ornament in an elite warrior's grave of the Viking Age, awaiting an interpretation that unlocks its secrets.

Though we are unlikely to get any solid proof of Wiligut's involvement with the Wewelsburg sun wheel, I take it as a given at this point. The alternate hypothesis, that Wiligut wasn't involved, defies belief. Considering the Wiligut ritual work that we know about, and Himmler's obsession with ritual and symbolism, why

---

[55] Flowers and Moynihan, *The Secret King*, 50–53, with citation of Hunger, *Die Runenkunde*, 164.

[56] Longerich, *Heinrich Himmler*, 287.

would Himmler neglect to make use of his top esotericist for such an important project as the North Tower?

The Historical Silence Regarding the Symbol's Meaning

Having settled upon Himmler and Wiligut as the men most likely responsible for the symbol, it's worth some moments to ask whether they told anybody about the design that I will argue for. The Nazis were famously bureaucratic, and Himmler especially so. While lots of documentation from the SS survives, we have nothing regarding the meaning that Himmler intended for the Wewelsburg sun wheel. Why should that be? This is speculative, but I'd like to suggest that the documentation may have never existed. Longerich makes a solid case and concludes that Himmler was being circumspect about various elements of his "new religion" for the SS and Germany, because Himmler felt they were not ready for it yet.[57] So it's entirely possible that Himmler and Wiligut told no one what the design meant, not even Bartels. Bartels and those responsible for installing the sun wheel may only have been told to put it there, thinking it was just a decorative ornament and not knowing its deeper meaning. I might literally be the third person ever to know what it really is, especially in the detail outlined here. Surprised? I will argue for the symbol's development at right around the same time that Wiligut was being ousted. That would not induce Himmler to immediately share any details about what he was working on with him! Instead, it might convince Himmler that it should wait a while before being introduced to its intended audience. After all, I also argue that the symbol and its meaning were only meant for a very small group of the most elite men, so that a certain amount of secrecy would likely go with it. Then, as the war heated up, sharing the details of this particular vision would have been added to the long list of matters that were postponed to await the final victory that never came.

---

[57] Longerich, *Heinrich Himmler*, 298.

Wiligut's Santur: Could a Black Sun Actually Be Involved?

Before we pursue what's really going on with the Wewelsburg symbol, I shall address whether any kind of black sun could be plausibly involved in all this. And only Wiligut is the potential vector for this material to get Himmler's attention and approval for putting it onto the floor of the Wewelsburg North Tower.

Wiligut indeed appears to have had esoteric doctrines about a "burned out" sun which he called Santur, a counterpart to the luminous sun we see today. But almost nothing of the surviving Santur material comes from Wiligut directly. Rather, we get it today via one of his students, Emil Rüdiger.[58] The material on Santur claims that it was still visible during the time of the Greek poet Homer, and though it is now invisible, it is still near planet Earth and emitting an influence. Most significant in the material is the vague claims that imply Santur could be invoked to provide beneficent influences that would enable modern-day Aryans to regain their former glories. It cannot be denied that such a notion would appeal to Himmler. But that is all we have. Other things are said about Santur, but literally none of it gives any grounds for seeing the Wewelsburg symbol as a depiction of Santur. The Santur material simply cannot account for *any* of the distinctive features of the symbol (whether rings, spokes, central circle, or core, none of which are actually black), nor why it should be put in a room resembling the *Parsifal* Grail Hall. In my view, this Santur Mythos is far too obscure for it to mythopoetically inspire the OGFs in Himmler's Holy of Holies. Not one of them would have ever heard of it before. Instead, I will suggest something that educated OGFs were far more likely to appreciate.

I recognize that many people (both for and against Nazis) want to believe that the symbol was for channeling obscure, occult, secret forces for enabling Aryan supremacy, and notions of a black sun certainly offer the kind of dark and lurid fantasy that those people are looking for. Yet that is the only extent to which I will entertain any discussion here of this symbol as a black sun. Those looking to explore the vast, sprawling black sun mythology

---

[58] Pontolillo, *The Black Sun Unveiled*, 303–18 (chapter on Wiligut), 319–35 (chapter on Rüdiger).

that became attached to the symbol starting in the 1990s should look to Pontolillo's books. Instead, I offer a different mythological nexus for this symbol, one that makes far more sense in the context of Wewelsburg and Himmler's ambitions to cultivate a warrior elite. It is one where I explain what the symbol *actually looks like*. And now, with the context for this symbol laid out—in both its location and the persons likely responsible for its design—I present the evidence and exhibits for my case: the materials I believe that Himmler and Wiligut actually drew upon in creating it, and these materials account for the *entirety* of its peculiar design.

Archaeological Antecedent: The Zierscheibe

Was the Wewelsburg sun wheel based on archaeological findings? That's a common observation these days. Goodrick-Clarke notes:

> It has been suggested that this twelve-spoke sun wheel derives from decorative disks of the Merovingians of the early medieval period and are supposed to represent the visible sun or its passage through the months of the year. These disks were discussed in scholarly publications during the Third Reich and may well have served the Wewelsburg designers as a model.[59]

And these sun wheel designs do seem to have been at least a minor fad during the Third Reich. There is at least one plastic badge from 1941 of a nine-spoked sun wheel with a swastika in the center, meant to look like the ancient designs.[60] An eight-spoked wheel, also with a swastika at the center, was found in a WWII wall painting in a military bunker in Hamburg, accompanied by text that read "The German race is young, strong, full of virtue and initiative. The Nordic peoples hear the Future calling."[61] That the Wewelsburg sun wheel should be connected to this trend seems quite reasonable. However, Siepe recognizes that "a connection has yet to be confirmed through reliable sources," but she does note that potential interpretations of these decorative disks "would fit

---

[59] Goodrick-Clarke, *Black Sun*, 148.

[60] John-Stucke, "Himmler's Plans," figure 1.12, 20, 30–31n91.

[61] Pontolillo, *The Black Sun Unveiled*, 45.

well into the SS's supposedly Germanic customs."⁶² So let us take a look at these archeological finds. Typically called Zierscheibe,⁶³ the finds in question are:

> Ornamental discs from the Merovingian period (5th–8th centuries), which were certainly not meant to symbolize an invisible sun, but rather the visible one. Graves from the early Middle Ages have yielded several variants of such ornamental discs, which were especially common in different regions of Central Europe, with their decoration ranging from equal-armed crosses to geometric and figurative elements.⁶⁴

Dorothee Renner published an extensive analysis of these discs.⁶⁵ Pontolillo cites five of the Type IIA examples from her book as the closest matches to the Wewelsburg sun wheel. He further notes that Hermann Wirth, leader of the SS Ahnenerbe at the time, described one of these discs in a 1936 publication, while all five of them "were in the possession of German museums and/or published in the archaeological literature prior to 1938." Here are the examples Pontolillo gives from Renner as most similar to the Wewelsburg sun wheel (not to scale):⁶⁶

Now we can precisely describe them, and then clearly see the large explanatory gap facing us. These Zierscheibe all have an *outer ring* and an *inner ring*. They have *sun-rune spokes*, but these vary from five to seven, which is a good deal short of the twelve in the Wewelsburg symbol. (Of course, the castle floor has room to fit

---

62 Siepe, "The Sun Wheel," 144.

63 This German word normally has a plural form of Zierscheiben. For the simplicity of my text, I will use Zierscheibe as both singular and plural.

64 Siepe, "The Sun Wheel," 144.

65 Renner, *Die durchbrochenen Zierscheiben der Merowingerzeit*.

66 Pontolillo, *The Black Sun Unveiled*, 47–48.

more spokes in, but why go up to twelve?) In the picture, they are variously the "regular" or "reversed" sun-rune form, but we shouldn't read anything into that. They are see-through objects that can be flipped either way. And there's no evidence that the directionality of the sun-rune made any difference to the peoples of that time. Beyond that, the spokes don't go into the empty centers, which have no central circle like the Wewelsburg symbol.

But there were far more Zierscheibe than those five, and just to make a supposal, let's consider the whole range of Zierscheibe pictured in Renner's text. Might there be a disk in there that sheds further light on the matter, even if it was one not discovered until after the Third Reich? That is, if we want to go down the road of "suppose the SS had some lost Zierscheibe that we don't know about." Do the Zierscheibe we know about today offer any potential room for reasonable speculation in this regard? Here are a few more from Renner's book:

There are some designs with an outer ring, a middle ring, and an inner ring, like 74 and 111 here. The spokes sometimes cross rings, but as seen in the examples just above, it is always inconsistent and random (and without an attempt at symmetry) as to whether a spoke from the middle ring to the inner ring is a direct continuation of a spoke from the outer ring. Number 97 is the only one to have a small central circle that isn't a ring. Among dozens and dozens in Renner's book that have sun-rune spokes, number 51 is literally the only one with deliberately lopsided arms —it is clearly an unnatural choice when making these designs. There is no help from the rest of the 699 items in Renner's book that have not already been shown. There is simply no precedent among them for the fat central circle and peculiar core of the Wewelsburg sun wheel. For these other Zierscheibe, it's not even worth checking whether there was any chance the SS saw them. They give nothing to the design beyond the five of Type IIA given above. *Maybe* number 51 would be license for unequal-armed spokes, but certainly not by itself. There would need to be an additional basis for choosing such a rare and unnatural design.

Ultimately, none of the Zierscheibe in Renner's book is a direct model for the Wewelsburg symbol. And I don't think any such direct model existed, so no, the SS did not have some lost Zierscheibe. We will do better to stick to the Type IIA Zierscheibe that we know were available to the SS in the 1930s. If the Wewelsburg symbol is somehow inspired by those Zierscheibe (I think it is), then we must account for the significant differences it has with them (and I will). But more importantly, how could a Zierscheibe design possibly be thought exceptional enough to place at the center of Himmler's Holy of Holies? Nobody bringing up the connection before now has attempted to answer that question. Pay especially close attention to the five- and six-spoked ones here among Type IIA. We will see a suprisingly similar design in a most unexpected context, one that would have surely fired the imaginations of Himmler and Wiligut, and it's a context that makes the Zierscheibe important enough for the North Tower. But now it is time for what I believe inspired Himmler and Wiligut to create the Wewelsburg symbol generally, and especially its peculiar center region.

The Vision of the Grail at the Round Table

Let us turn to the High Middle Ages and the great romances of King Arthur, the Knights of the Round Table, and the Holy Grail. The story has many versions. The relevant one here is called the Lancelot-Grail cycle, consisting of several books (as we would now think of "books"). In one of these, *The Quest for the Holy Grail* (*Queste del Saint Graal*), and in the first chapter, Arthur and his knights are gathered at the Round Table, celebrating Pentecost. In radiant glory, the Grail appears before them, fills the table with a wondrous feast, and then vanishes.[67] The vision inspires the knights to start questing to find and return the Holy Grail. This image of the Grail appearing before the Round Table was very captivating and inspiring for audiences, since at least three late medieval manuscripts have illuminations depicting this scene, and

---

[67] Comfort, *The Quest of the Holy Grail*, 19.

very similarly. I picture only the first of them here (the most important one for my argument), which is by Maître des Clères Femmes in a manuscript of the text from circa 1406.[68] The other two were both created by Évrard d'Espinques later in that century. They are in manuscripts from circa 1470 and circa 1475.[69] Though they have their differences, they are quite similar, and one suspects that Évrard based his illuminations on Maître's, though I won't pursue that here. Here is Maître's illumination:

One will readily notice that this illumination has several distinctive features. First, while the Round Table has an *outer edge* like all tables do, it also has an *inner edge*, such that there is a *central hole* inside the inner edge of the table. Second, the *Grail* is floating above this central hole in the table, and shining with a *radiant halo* that looks to fill most of the space of the central hole. These first two points are especially critical for my analysis. The number of knights depicted here is 10. (The features of the Round Table and Grail just mentioned are the same in Évrard's illuminations, which

---

[68] BnF Manuscrits Français 120 folio 524v. The artist name is a conventional designation for a Dutch illuminator or workshop operating in Paris from around 1403 to 1415. A number of works are attributed to this person, but the actual artist or artists remain anonymous.

[69] Respectively, BnF Manuscrits Français 112, folio 5r and BnF Manuscrits Français 116, folio 610v. These images are all available from the online *Gallica Digital Library*, see the works cited section.

show 21 or 15 knights, respectively.) This image, by itself, might be just enough to argue for the identity of the Wewelsburg sun wheel, though it may seem a stretch. But there are more Round Tables, and they reinforce the distinctive features mentioned above and greatly strengthen the case beyond that.

The Winchester Roundtable

At Winchester Castle in Winchester, Hampshire, England, there hangs a large wooden table believed to have been made during the reign of King Edward I (1272–1307), for a tournament that he held. It was repainted during the reign of King Henry VIII (1509–1547). Here is a picture of it:[70]

King Arthur is depicted here, and around the edge of the table are the names of 24 of his knights. I draw attention to the distinctive features this table shares with the manuscript image discussed just above. There is a clearly marked *outer edge* to this Round Table,

---

[70] "King Arthur's Round Table at Winchester," *Wikimedia Commons*. Photo by Rs-nourse.

and also a clearly marked *inner edge*. The table has a *central space* in the middle. But instead of the Grail, we have a double-rose motif occupying that central space—the white rose at the center with a red rose around it (or just the white rose and its own core) makes a striking parallel to the Grail and its halo. The alternating green and white color scheme divides the table quite strikingly into different sections running from the outer edge to the inner edge.

The Round Table in the *Wigalois* of Wirnt von Grafenberg

Among the lesser-known Arthurian texts is *Wigalois* by the Middle High German poet Wirnt von Grafenberg. This epic tells the adventures of Gawain's son. But it is a particular *Wigalois* manuscript itself that is most significant here. Produced in 1372, this manuscript, LTK 537, is in the collection of the Leiden University Libraries. Just before folio 1 of the manuscript, there is the following image of the Round Table:[71]

---

[71] LTK 537, opening 4.

Though far less striking than the previous two images (this one is actually quite dismal, and the markings give the impression the illumination was left unfinished), the reader by now undoubtedly sees where I'm going with this. Despite the roughness of the image, the distinctive features are quite noticeable. An ink circle marks the *outer edge* of the table, and another marks the *inner edge.* In the *central hole*, there is a small *gold disk* in the middle. But why should there be a small gold disk in the center of this Round Table? Is it the Grail? That certainly can't be concluded from the image alone, nor its position at the beginning of the manuscript. Does the text itself offer any clues? It does not. Though *Wigalois* is an Arthurian romance, it is not a Grail story, and the Grail is not in it at all. There does not appear to be a definitive answer anywhere, since an entire recent scholarly book on the use of ekphrasis in *Wigalois* can only say "perhaps a platter?" about that gold disk in the middle.[72] It appears this image is simply a general depiction of the Round Table with which to preface the story—after all, Arthur and the Round Table are repeatedly mentioned throughout—but it is not inspired by any particular scene in the text. But it may be making some allusions. This Round Table is peculiar and unlike any other pre-modern depictions, for it has six swords laid upon the table, all pointing toward the middle. James Brown (who instead sees these as knives) considers this as an allusion to the Wheel of Fortune motif (in that the swords' positioning is reminiscent of the spokes of a wheel) which occurs repeatedly in the text and other illuminations in the manuscript, and even a deliberate conflation of the two—that is, that this illumination is meant to be seen as both the Round Table and the Wheel of Fortune.[73]

Wigalois and the Wheel of Fortune

There are other illuminations in the manuscript that depict the Wheel of Fortune, and there is something very peculiar about them. Wigalois has a Wheel of Fortune charge on his shield, and

---

[72] Brown, *Imagining the Text*, 144.

[73] Brown, *Imagining the Text*, 144–45, 251.

in this manuscript, there are *twenty-eight* separate illuminations that feature this design. Here is one of those illuminations:[74]

As may be seen in this example, the Wheel of Fortune devices vary in the number of spokes they have. Six is most common, though five occurs frequently, but those are the only numbers of spokes it is depicted with. The design is quite striking in that it has an outer ring, an inner ring, and spokes connecting the two, although there is never anything depicted inside the inner ring in these.

As a heraldic device, it is also used by Gawain, Wigalois' father, and the text itself conflates it by calling it a golden Round Table when Lady Beleare describes it:

> I was a child when I saw him, and the tournament took place at my father's castle. He had come from King Arthur seeking knightly sport. He was brave and strong, and was named Sir Gawain. On his shield was a golden Round Table, so fashioned that no one ever saw an emblem as splendid. Painted on it with chalk, believe me, was a white stag on a golden mountain, the coat of arms of him who captured all the knights. The Table which encircled it was worn by no knight, so I have heard, except him who with great labor and courage had won a place there. Whoever succeeded in this wore the Round Table so that one could know that he had a seat there.[75]

---

[74] LTK 537, folio 36v.

[75] Wirnt, *Wigalois* (trans.), 166–67.

This is indeed an appropriation of the Wheel of Fortune as a symbol of the Round Table, as Neil Thomas' commentary on this passage helps make clear:

> This conception of the symbols of Fortune having become little more than Arthurian trophies is reinforced when the Lady Beleare recollects having once seen not the Wheel of Fortune but (as she interprets it) 'the golden Round Table' ('guldîn tavelrunde', line 5613) as Gawein's emblem before she noticed it on Wigalois's shield (it is this which enables her to tell the son's identity).[76]

The text has another cue that links that design to the Round Table just a little later on, when Wigalois is getting ready for a battle:

> His host wanted to give him a shield made of a griffin's claw to help him in the adventure, but the knight would not accept it, and they brought him his own shield. He took it because it showed that he was a knight of the Round Table.[77]

The net result of this is that the manuscript is declaring that this Wheel of Fortune device in the illuminations is also a direct symbol of the Round Table and its Knights, depicting the outer and inner edges of the round table, connected by spokes. The text doesn't tell us how we should see those spokes. But the Round Table illumination at the beginning of the manuscript offers a basis for thinking of them as swords, given that it may be read as an enlarged view of the small Wheel of Fortune sigils in the rest of the manuscript.

But more importantly, the reader of this essay will have also noticed that these Wheel of Fortune illuminations bear a striking resemblance to the Zierscheibe with their outer and inner rings and connecting spokes. And for my purposes here, it is not the Wheel of Fortune that matters, but that a Zierschiebe-like symbol is equated with the Round Table.

---

[76] Thomas, *Wirnt von Gravenberg's Wigalois*, 52.

[77] Wirnt, *Wigalois* (trans.), 172–73. "His own shield": that is, the one with the Wheel of Fortune design.

Art Imitates Unknown Prior Art

Here, I make a short digression, but one that helps illustrate part of my interpretation. Though it postdates the SS by nearly 70 years, a very striking modern image must be mentioned. It is from the mobile game *Kingdoms of Camelot: Battle for the North*, which was released in March 2012 by the studio and publisher Kabam (named Watercooler, Inc. at the time).[78] Its loading screen features an iconic image. In 2018, it became a meme that has since spawned countless variations, and this meme is now typically referred to as "Swords United."[79] Here I show the original picture, plus one of the many meme variants:[80]

The original picture shows three people, a king and two knights, holding their swords pointed toward the center of a table. Nine additional swords also point inward, held by hands unseen and offscreen, making for a total of twelve swords and knights. Though not labeled, this image is obviously meant to be King Arthur and the Knights of the Round Table. In meme usage, the center of the table is labeled with some cause or other, and the swords around

---

[78] "*Kingdoms of Camelot*," *Wikipedia*.

[79] "Swords United," *Meming Wiki*; "Swords United," *Know Your Meme*.

[80] Both images are from "Swords United," *Meming Wiki*.

the table are labeled with various persons or factions that have united in support of that cause. For my purposes, it would be quite appropriate to compare that center-item in the memes to the Grail—thus it is some Grail or other that the meme is meant to show people uniting around. This image is popular beyond just memes. It is also depicted in painted resin statuary with the full round table and the knights holding their swords in the middle, most commonly with twelve knights at the table, sometimes thirteen.[81]

These various "Swords United" depictions—both the game image and the statues—do look related in some fashion, as they depict the Round Table with distinctive Celtic knotwork. As all of these "Swords United" style images postdate the SS by many decades, it would serve no purpose to trace the flow of influence between them. But it would be natural to wonder if the *Wigalois* illumination was the inspiration for this. It is unlikely in the extreme. There appears to be no connection in art style, and *Wigalois* is frankly too obscure outside of Germany. So I can only hypothesize that "Swords United" is a modern, spontaneous manifestation of the symbol of the Round Table. Thus, I reckon the *Wigalois* Round Table illumination as kind of "proto" Swords United. But the twenty-first-century depictions do show an important detail: namely, in the modern world, if you're going to depict the Knights of the Round Table, twelve (or occasionally thirteen) seems to be the most natural number of knights for such a depiction.

As for medieval works that would point to twelve or thirteen as a symbolic number of knights for the Round Table (and perhaps a source for Swords United or anyone else), Robert de Boron's cycle of Arthurian Romances from the thirteenth century indicates the Round Table is fashioned after the table of the Last Supper and of the Grail Table of Joseph of Arimathea. And it has Arthur say "The twelve peers of my court will sit in the twelve seats" of the Round Table, and it is noted that the thirteenth seat remained

---

[81] See "Resin Statuary Examples" in the works cited for some links.

empty, symbolizing Judas.[82] There can hardly be any need to seek other early sources on the matter, which clearly corresponds the Knights of the Round Table to the Apostles, who are famously twelve themselves.

The Grail: The Color Green from Wolfram

The greatest of the medieval Grail epics is surely Wolfram von Eschenbach's *Parzival*, and it is German. As with *Wigalois*, it probably got special attention from the SS on that account. I believe Wolfram's account contributes an important detail to the Wewelsburg sun wheel. Though never mentioning the color of the Grail itself, Wolfram says the Grail is presented on a green silk cloth:

> Upon a green achmardi she carried the perfection of Paradise, both root and branch. This was a thing that was called the Grail, earth's perfection's transcendence.[83]

It also seems to be a popular idea that the Grail is a green stone, although there does not seem to be a specific source for this belief. Perhaps it is a conflation of medieval traditions connecting green stones to renewal, divine wisdom, or the alchemical philosopher's stone. But Wolfram gives us the critical piece here: the Grail is most properly displayed by putting it in a green setting of some kind.

Wiligut's Reversed Sun-Runes

Though commentators are generally now noticing that the sun-rune spokes on the Wewelsburg sun wheel are, in fact, *reversed* from the ordinary sun-rune shape, nobody seems to have attempted to explain why, let alone look into the esoteric runology of Karl Maria Wiligut to see what it might say about such runes. After all, whether or not one thinks he designed the Wewelsburg symbol directly, Wiligut actually has an esoteric runology with a

---

[82] Robert de Boron, *Merlin and the Grail*, 1–2, 112, 116. This translation is based on the Modena manuscript containing the trilogy of *Joseph of Arimathea*, *Merlin*, and *Perceval*.

[83] Wolfram, *Parzival and Titurel*, 99–100 (Book V, §235).

reversed sun-rune, and he was a close confidant of Himmler on occult matters, making him the only plausible candidate for imbuing the symbol with a meaning for such reversed runes. The ordinary sun-rune shape is the Sig-rune of the SS (and also of Guido von List and Wiligut), and it has its origin in the sun-rune shape Sól of the Viking Age and the Younger Futhark. But there is nothing in that historical origin to suggest any special meaning for "reversed" runes—they are merely the same as the ordinary-direction version of the rune.

That the sun-runes of the Wewelsburg symbol are indeed reversed from the ordinary Sig-rune used in the SS logo would have been obvious to everyone, most especially Himmler himself. But why not use the ordinary Sig-rune? After all, it was very distinctive of the SS. Let's see what Wiligut had to say about the reversed Sig rune, which he calls Zil. In an article in the ariosophical journal *Hagal*, Wiligut (under the pen name Jarl Widar) outlines his esoteric runology. (I pointed out above the evidence that Wiligut had sent Himmler a draft of this!) Here is the relevant portion concerning the Sig and Zil runes:

> Im Al das Gotosfeuer von Geist im Stoff durch kraft—
> Zeigt "sig-sal-sol-sun-rune", der Schöpfung Meisterschaft . . .
> Dämonisch umgewendet erscheint sie uns als Zil
> Als zag und zug—das endet, zur Ru das Lebenspiel . . .
>
> In the Al Gotos' fire of Spirit in Matter demonstrates—
> Through Energy the "sig-sal-sol-sun-rune," and mastery of creation . . .
> Demoniacally inverted it appears to us as Zil,
> As zig and zag—this ends the game of life in rest . . .[84]

Regarding Zil, the translators indicate in their text that it is an alternate spelling for Ziel, "target; aim; goal." Specifically, it is a Middle High German spelling, and Wiligut uses more of them in his jargon, and educated Germans of the day would have rough familiarity with MHG through their schooling.[85] I am uncertain

---

[84] Wiligut, "Gotos Raunen—Runenwissen!" 13. The translation is from Flowers and Moynihan, *The Secret King*, 93. I have changed the line breaks in the translation to more closely match the original German.

[85] Personal correspondence with Flowers and Moynihan.

what to make of Wiligut's riddle regarding these runes—and it is very much a riddling passage—except to connect it to the warrior who has fallen in battle striving for his aim, and thus finally has earned his rest. Alternatively, one may think of Sir Galahad in some versions of the Grail Quest, who after attaining the Grail, immediately dies in supreme delight and is carried off to heaven. Ultimately, I must concede that I'm not certain what to make of *dämonisch* (demoniacally) here. If the reader is inclined to find it unacceptable, perhaps the only way out is to conclude that these sun-rune spokes were not meant to be seen as runes at all, but simply as swords (which I discuss below, and which is not affected by whether or not one thinks the spokes are runes). But that view would deprive the symbol of what I fall back on here most, which is the rich meaning of the name Zil itself as "target; aim; goal." And what we have on the floor of the North Tower are twelve runes all meaning aim or goal that are pointing directly at that *core* where the gold disk was reputed to be. They are meant to emphasize that the gold disk represents a supremely important goal or objective.

The Perfect Storm in 1938

The reader is certainly wondering by now if I'm going to suggest that Himmler and Wiligut saw the preceding medieval images, and how that possibly could have happened. After all, there was no internet in the early twentieth century, and these images are in diverse sources across time and space. We can look them up now easily, but finding them in the 1930s would have been quite a challenge. But yes, I'm arguing they did indeed see them, and all of them in a single place.

This story turns now to Roger Sherman Loomis (1887–1966), an American scholar and one of the foremost authorities on all things Arthurian in his day. He published many books on the Arthurian legends. In 1938, along with his wife, he published *Arthurian Legends in Medieval Art*. What a sensation this book must have made at the time! Loomis had read and studied broadly all the Arthurian art he could find and wrote a treatise on it, complete with reproductions of *over four hundred* pieces of medieval art, each of which gets a bit of discussion. They are conveniently numbered, and figures 287, 18, and 367 are The Vision of the Grail, The Winchester Roundtable, and the Wigalois Round Table, respectively, and figure 369 is one of four Wigalois Wheel of Fortune sigil depictions in the book—yes, all the same images discussed above! This is how they appear in the book (although they are smaller here), where they would have been seen by the designers of the Wewelsburg sun wheel:

Just as a close associate brought Rahn's book on the Grail to the attention of Himmler and Wiligut, surely someone did the same for the Loomis book. They must have been quite delighted to see it! This was an enormous treasure trove of Arthurian art to sift through for their ceremonial and ritual purposes. These images in the Loomis book are in black and white, so they would not have yet seen the gold disk of the *Wigalois* illumination there. But of the three key images I'm discussing, that one is in the Netherlands, at Leiden, and Loomis even says so right in the text of the book.[86] But even before making any kind of research inquiry to Leiden, their appetites would be whetted further by a text they could easily obtain. That was one of the printed editions of *Wigalois* available at the time: the 1819 edition by George Friederich Benecke, published in Berlin.[87] In it, Benecke describes the Leiden manuscript, LTK 537, saying:

> Die Handschrift ist mit vielen Bildern geziert, die gewöhnlich eine halbe, bisweilen auch eine ganze Seite einnehmen, und an denen weniger das Gold als die Kunst des Zeichners gespart ist.
>
> The manuscript is decorated with many pictures, which usually take up half a page, sometimes a whole page, and in which far more gold is used than the artist has skill for.[88]

In his glossary, Benecke gives a tantalizing entry for the Round Table that serves as a strong nudge to any readers who may have been uncertain about connecting it to the Wheel of Fortune sigil:

> Diu tavel runde . . . an der an Artus Hofe die Riter saßen, und welche in Gold auf ihrem Schilde um ihr Wapen stand.
>
> The round table . . . at which the knights sat at Arthur's court, and which stood in gold on their shields around their coats of arms.[89]

---

[86] "This manuscript, now in Leyden (Bibl. der Ryks-Univ. No. 537), is remarkable in several ways." Loomis, *Arthurian Art*, 134.

[87] There were at least two other editions of *Wigalois* available at the time, a 1926 edition by J. M. N. Kapteyn and an 1847 edition by Franz Pfeiffer. Though none of these three editions discusses the Round Table illumination at the beginning of the Leiden manuscript, it is my view that Benecke's edition offers the most tantalizing enticement for Himmler and Wiligut to seek out the manuscript.

[88] Wirnt, *Wigalois* (ed.), xxxviii. Translation mine.

[89] Wirnt, *Wigalois* (ed.), 719. Translation mine.

Between the Loomis book and Benecke's edition, Himmler and Wiligut were undoubtedly eager to get a full report on the Leiden manuscript of this *German* text, where they would have been struck by the gold disk in the Wigalois Round Table illumination and the excessive use of Zierschiebe-like designs to represent the Round Table. For a man as powerful as Himmler, getting all that would only take a few orders and phone calls to make it happen. At the end of this, the Wheel of Fortune images would easily be a basis for Wiligut to construe the Zierscheibe as little depictions of the Round Table. This was no stretch for him; rather, it would be entirely consistent with his *modus operandi* as revealed in Dechend's zodiac anecdote.

Putting It All Together: The Mystery Solved

Having presented all of my evidence and exhibits, I offer my explanation of the design of the iconic Wewelsburg symbol and its rationale as follows:

1. The Vision of the Grail illumination is the main template for the symbol, with its outer and inner edges corresponding to the outer and inner rings of the symbol. The Grail is the core of the symbol, and the Grail's halo is the central circle of the symbol, and thus the central hole is accounted for.
2. The Winchester Round Table's main contribution is the striking division of the symbol into equal portions for each knight represented (though it shows 24 knights), which is done via swords in the Wewelsburg symbol. Beyond this, the Winchester Round Table reinforces the use of a clearly marked outer and inner edge to the table, and the idea of putting a special doublet (the white and red roses here correspond to the symbol's core and central circle) in the central hole.
3. The Wigalois Round Table contributes the use of swords on the symbol (wonderful martial imagery for Himmler), as well as the use of a golden disk at the center for the Grail, alluding to stories in which the Grail is a platter or serving dish. This Round Table also reinforces a clearly marked outer and inner edge, plus having something special in the central hole.

4. The Wigalois Wheel of Fortune sigil, having been construed as a symbol of the Round Table itself, is then taken as license for seeing the Zierscheibe as early depictions of the Round Table and its legends! This provides the impulse for Himmler and Wiligut to create the ultimate Zierscheibe Round Table design.
5. Wiligut's runology is brought in with the Wigalois Round Table and Zierscheibe imagery to sanction the use of Zil-rune spokes in the symbol to represent the swords of twelve knights. This represents the unity of the knights joining together in pursuit and defense of the Grail, which is the ultimate goal, appropriate on account of Zil's meaning as target, aim, or goal, and all 12 of the spokes pointing straight at the Grail. The short arm of each rune is the hilt, the horizontal is the guard, and the long arm is the blade, and this accounts for the peculiar and deliberate lopsidedness of these Zil runes, which is *almost never* seen in historical Zierscheibe. All this comes out of a deliberate desire to make the whole symbol look like a Zierscheibe (they see them as little Round Tables, after all!) and incorporate Zil symbolism. If there were not this desire, they could have simply used a device that looked more directly like a sword, such as this dagger glyph or other non-stylistic image: †. We may also think of the sword-spokes as the knights drawing strength from the Grail, for their swords touch its halo.
6. Twelve spokes are used instead of 24 (the sections of the Winchester Round Table), probably out of a desire to allude to significant instances of the number 12, and simply because 24 swords in the symbol would have made it look too overloaded. Also, the SS was organized into 12 main offices by 1942, and one suspects that number to be a deliberate choice by Himmler. As discussed above, 12 sits comfortably as an appropriate minimum of knights for signifying the Round Table. Finally, Wiligut's zodiac fascination likely contributed to using 12 as a number to signify the zodiac and the solar wheel.

7. The lost gold disk that was sitting in the center of the Wewelsburg sun wheel was literally the Holy Grail for Himmler, something important enough to put at his Center of the World! And so the rest of the Sun Wheel was made green (along with the sandstone columns in the hall), since green is Wolfram's proper color for displaying the Grail.

Now, after over 80 years, there is a complete explanation for the symbol's design. Some may object that this is rather syncretic. But when have Himmler and Wiligut ever *not* been so? Or they may object on the grounds of the relative absence of evidence regarding Himmler having an abiding personal fascination with Grail and Arthurian matters. It's unnecessary to think that he did in order to accept my argument here. As seen above, there's enough material to show Himmler was adequately aware of the Grail Mythos. And he was an eminently practical man, and his "new religion" project was everywhere piecemeal. The OGF Hall, the Gruft, the Death's Head rings, the SS seasonal celebrations & personal rites (not to mention Wiligut's astrology and runology), and more are all over the map. It would be very strange to insist that Himmler had some abiding thematic interest regarding any of them, and one would be unlikely to find such. Each thing is its own whole, and without any *common theme*, making use of whatever seemed useful in each circumstance. We have the Round Table and Grail for the OGF Hall, then probably something to do with the roots of the World Tree for the Gruft, the varied elements of the Death's Head rings, and so on for the rest. Instead, Himmler's guiding star is the single *common purpose* of cultivating a warrior elite through a multitude of measures both great and small. It is that common purpose that is the only true unifier in Himmler's grand schemes for Wewelsburg, for which he chose an icon of Round Table to grace one of the most significant rooms of the castle.

The function of this Round Table symbol is fairly straightforward:
1. All of the sources, blueprints, and developments suggest that the entire North Tower was ultimately intended as a dedicated ceremonial and ritual space for the SS elite. Important meetings of the OGFs would perhaps be possible in it (like the June 1941 meeting, though the room was not

ready by then), to impart an air of sacrality to such proceedings. But mundane meetings of mid-level bureaucrats discussing things like arms manufacture or supply chains would surely be too low for such a venue.
2. Himmler put the Round Table symbol on the floor of the OGF Hall to impress upon the OGFs that they were a warrior elite on par with the greatest such elite of legend, Arthur's Knights of the Round Table, and that they had a sacred trust to seek and guard, namely the Grail itself. This was the ultimate extent of "the responsibility they bore before German history." The symbol is thus one mechanism among others—although surely the most iconic one—for Himmler to effectuate the ideological training of OGFs. Ceremony or ritual in the OGF Hall to this effect would have been developed eventually, but doubtlessly was cut short by the fall of the castle to the Allies.
3. The symbol was never meant for the masses. It was for the elite of the SS only. That is why it appeared nowhere else in Nazi Germany, and certainly would never have been put on banners for parade like the swastika was. (Though perhaps after the intended "Final Victory" it would have been an insignia for the SS elite to identify themselves as members of Himmler's new Round Table?)

Here is my timeline for its creation:
1. Himmler's 1937 speech in which he mentions hanging coats-of-arms in the not-yet-rebuilt Gruppenführer Hall shows that he has already been planning a glorious future for the North Tower.
2. In 1938, while Himmler and Wiligut are considering the future of the North Tower, the Loomis book is published and is brought to their attention, and they follow up on its leads, most likely prior to the start of the war in September 1939. After that, they design the Wewelsburg sun wheel. My sense is that it was Himmler who specifically wanted a Round Table design for his aims, while it was Wiligut who put together the iconography. The design of the symbol may or may not have run over into Wiligut's retirement.

3. In 1941, renovations began in earnest on the North Tower, and the sun wheel is installed prior to the halting of renovations in 1944, due to the demands of the war.

A Restatement: The Three Layers of the Symbol's Meaning

I consider the symbol to have three layers of meaning in light of the above:

1. First and foremost, the symbol is a depiction of the Round Table, the swords of 12 knights, and the Grail at the center with its halo. This is the primary meaning, because only this can account for all of the distinctive features of the symbol and their deviation from the Zierscheibe exemplars, and only this can offer an explanation for why Himmler would put it in the middle of his Holy of Holies.
2. On the secondary layer of meaning, it is a sun wheel just like the other Zierscheibe. Himmler and Wiligut were probably aware that the choice of 12 spokes would reinforce viewing this as a solar symbol. And the Arthurian and Grail stories are a solar mythos, after all. But this layer must be secondary, because "sun wheel" by itself cannot explain the distinctive features of the symbol or offer a rationale for putting it on the North Tower floor.
3. The third layer of meaning would be the things that random viewers of the symbol might potentially attribute to it. Some of these may or may not be intended by the designers, and all of them probably revolve around the number 12. On account of the Dechend anecdote and Wiligut's astrological material, I suspect that at least Wiligut himself considered the zodiac to be one of the most important "twelves" for the symbol, whereas Himmler surely appreciated the correspondence to the number of SS main offices. And 12 as the number of the highest-ranking Knights of the Round Table has its source in Robert de Boron's Arthurian cycle. But to be clear, other such third-layer meanings beyond these—for instance, twelve Aesir on their judgment seats in the *Edda*—border on the realm of pure speculation, whereas the previous twelves and the first two levels of meaning are firmly grounded interpretations.

Some Notable Implications of All This

1. I give the simplest, yet most profound and in-hindsight-obvious explanation for why the OGF Hall looks like the *Parsifal* Grail Hall: because it was meant to house the Grail!
2. Himmler really did have a Round Table, like others have claimed. It just wasn't the physical table that everyone was looking for. The real, iconic one has been right under our noses for decades and hasn't moved an inch in all that time.
3. The Wewelsburg sun wheel is effectively an OG edition of the "Swords United" meme, roughly 70 years prior to the aforementioned *Kingdoms of Camelot* game.[90] The game designers and meme makers surely had no clue that the idea had been done before. But yes, when you use the "Swords United" meme, you're using something that's a fairly exact equivalent to the Wewelsburg sun wheel.
4. The symbol was never a Nazi or fascist symbol in any sense: it never represented Nazi ideology or policies. It was never meant to be seen by the masses, but now it has! Instead, it was intended as a challenge for the OGFs to live up to, and it can be that challenge to us today as well. The Round Table and Grail are superior and anterior to petty modern political ideologies.
5. Following the above, it is clear that many people have been abusing or condemning what is really an Arthurian symbol. I consider such abuse or condemnation to be spiritually dangerous. Why? Much of our culture is extremely enchanted with the Arthurian Mythos, so viciously denigrating or abusing a symbol of one of its central mysteries at the same time can only produce deep contradiction and psychological ill health.
6. In light of my interpretation, many (most?) of the uses of the so-called "Black Sun" in recent decades look rather ridiculous. Most of those using it are clearly not worthy of

---

[90] "OG" is the common abbreviation for the colloquial phrase "Original Gangster," used to identify the earliest, authentic version of something, especially if it's long before it was popular. Doubtless, Himmler would not approve of the phrase.

the Round Table, let alone the Grail. Identifying and mocking such examples is left as an exercise for the reader.

Critiquing Faulty Depictions

Now that we know what it really is, one can better appreciate the ways in which most depictions of the symbol in pop culture are flawed vis-à-vis the original. Look around at the examples on the internet. It's clear that most people depicting this symbol are not that interested in making an accurate reproduction of what's actually on the floor of Wewelsburg's North Tower. Many more get the symbol wrong than get it right. There are two common flaws:

1. Lacking the Grail and/or the halo. Many casual depictions don't really have a central circle; instead, they just have the sword spokes of the wheel merely meeting in the center. Thus they depict "Swords United," but with no Grail in the middle! It's appropriate for them, because their wrong depiction drains the symbol of one of its most important and powerful aspects. Some get the central circle right, but include no distinctive core. Almost no one gets both the central circle and core completely correct, and so they don't get the full power of the Grail through its use.
2. Depictions that have relatively equal-armed sun-rune spokes, which reduce the intended sword effect. Such depictions are *extremely* common. They show that if you don't know these are supposed to be swords, it is a natural tendency to make the sun-rune spokes equal-armed.

No real central circle Diminished sword aspect

Both short spokes and no central circle

Generally good, only missing the Grail core

These account for the vast majority of the flawed depictions. I must wonder, has the higher nature of the symbol cast a reality distortion field upon most who look at it, such that they can't get it right? Undoubtedly, the neo-nazi fanbois who use this symbol will continue to use the various defective forms and the symbol's wrong name, and that's probably for the best. Thus, all the "Black Sun" nonsense has produced a positive effect after all, and perhaps one intended by Spirit, in drawing away those who could not become worthy of true challenge the symbol represents. But how might the esoterically inclined who seek the Grail properly name and depict the symbol going forward?

Re-Naming the Symbol

It is time to retire the label of "Black Sun" as a name for this particular symbol. I myself no longer call it that. (This is not to disparage the very real and important occult doctrines regarding black suns, which are quite independent of anything to do with Nazi Germany. People should just stop associating them with this symbol.) Though I'm confident in the correctness of my explanation, I suspect the Nazi-obsessed cultures (both for and against) will continue to call it a "Black Sun" for quite a while. Against that, I now offer proper names for the symbol, and all with German translations to go with them:

- **The so-called "Black Sun"** (Die sogenannte „Schwarze Sonne"). As the wrong attribution to a black sun is sadly how

most people know this symbol, the form given here should be used when there is a need to refer to how it was commonly known at the time of this publication, in order to emphasize that it is a false name. Yes, use this name exactly as given, quotation marks and all, to emphasize its falsity. You'll notice that I included it in this essay's title.
- **Round Table Ornamental Disk** (Tafelrunde Zierscheibe). The German of this may have been what the Himmler and Wiligut themselves called the symbol. This is probably not to be recommended to English speakers, as we are not used to saying "ornamental disk" to refer to either the Wewelsburg symbol or the Zierscheibe, though that is the proper translation of the latter. But whatever one's opinion on the Zierscheibe portion, I think it highly likely that "Tafelrunde" was part of its proper name.
- **Round Table Sun Wheel** (Tafelrunde Sonnenrad). This name is perhaps the most compact expression possible of the two primary meanings of the symbol. To the extent that the SS was ever throwing around the term "Sonnenrad," this is also a potential original name for it. And this is the name I recommend for today and use myself. As it does not have the baggage that "Black Sun" has accumulated, it may help liberate this symbol from those who would abuse it or condemn it.

Depicting the Symbol Going Forward

Along with a different name for it, I also advocate depictions appropriate to its identity as the Round Table Sun Wheel. That is, for those who are ready to leave the fascist and anti-fascist nonsense behind and elevate themselves and others by using it as a tool to invoke the Round Table and Grail. That means adhering to the actual design seen on the Wewelsburg floor through primarily these two points:
1. Getting the proportions of the Zil runes at least approximately correct in recognition of their identity as swords.
2. A properly sized central circle with a distinctive core to depict the Grail and its halo.

Here is an example in three different color schemes:[91]

For Black & White Use

Suggestion for Jewelry

Castle-Floor Style

The first is suitable for monochrome print use. The third aims to approximate the colors of the original with its lost gold disk, but this is difficult in monotones, as the mottled-green marble of the original varies quite a bit in its shades of green, running from relatively light to almost black. The second one draws on the

---

[91] These images are remixes of "Black Sun," *Wikimedia Commons*, by the user Blacksonne (shown just previously as the "generally good" example), which is under a CC BY-SA 4.0 license as indicated in the works cited. I have changed the colors and added a core to each of them. These remixes are thus also under a CC BY-SA 4.0 license, and digital versions are available at Westcoat, *The Skaldic Eagle*.

identity as a sun wheel and the notion of the Grail as a green stone, and one might envision this as a pendant made of gold with an emerald or moldavite in the middle. I have kept the number of different colors here to a minimum, but others might try experimenting with a broader palette and color individual elements according to taste.

Liberating the Round Table Sun Wheel: Why Now & Me?

I won't try to recount the endless uses of this symbol under the moniker of the so-called "Black Sun." Suffice it to say that the vast majority of uses are wholly inappropriate for what is actually an amazingly beautiful and elegant symbol of Arthur's Round Table and the Holy Grail. It is time this Arthurian symbol was liberated from the neo-nazis who abuse it, and the antifa who condemn it as some white supremacist symbol that it never was.

All should realize that the great powers Himmler invoked in the North Tower as an axis mundi and the seat of the Round Table and Grail did not save the SS and the Nazis from defeat. In their monstrosity, tyranny, and mass murder, the SS clearly did not learn the spiritual lessons that the Grail epics have left for those who would be worthy of the Grail. (Using concentration camp labor for remodeling that North Tower certainly didn't help!) But nor did the higher powers they invoked permit the Round Table Sun Wheel to be destroyed. Appropriately, despite the war, the attempted destruction of the castle when the SS abandoned it, the looting by locals, the occupation by the Allies, and the whole post-war period, this superlative symbol of the Round Table survives right where it has been for over 80 years, for no one could bring themselves to strike against it. Yes, despite all the post-war hand-wringing, no one could move to dismantle it. The Holy Grail and the Round Table are simply more powerful than both Nazism and its opponents, and very much so.

In both a physical and spiritual sense, the Grail departed from Wewelsburg to return to the realm of legend. As the physical gold disk hasn't surfaced after all this time, it was probably lost, melted down, or otherwise destroyed. It was no prize to be claimed by the victorious Allied forces, a warning that "our side" was not worthy of the Grail either. Only a nondescript, off-looking marble core remains in its place, as if it had never been. And in the post-war period, it was not given to the Nazis nor to the Anti-Nazis to uncover the true meaning of the Wewelsburg symbol. The higher world of Tradition kept this Round Table and Grail shrouded in mystery for nearly 80 years.

Why did the gods grace me with this opportunity to solve an 80-year-old mystery? Perhaps it is a sign that I've become, like Parzival, a "pure fool" who can walk the sword bridge and appropriately ask the Question. One who can quest for the Grail qua Grail, and not with an ideological axe to grind. And it is a sign that I'm one of the few who can delve into this matter of SS occultism dispassionately, without falling into the trap of fanaticism, whether pro- or anti-Nazi.[92] It is quite clear that many who do look as I did become fanatics. Both Nazis and Anti-Nazis will be furious that it was someone like me, and not someone on their side, who solved this mystery.

I am neither fascist nor anti-fascist. Instead, I am a secret third thing. I am many secret third things, for my god Óðinn is a god of secret third things. I should also add, and partly restate, by saying that I'm one of those people who is not that interested in Nazis qua Nazis one way or another. What I am interested in is the Grail Mythos, and I credit that Quest for leading me to this particular Grail.[93] But I am far from the first such occultist to look into this symbol with the necessary level of detachment. Besides Aquino, many other occultists have visited Wewelsburg and looked at the symbol,[94] but none appear to have seen the Round Table and Grail shining back at them. I can't claim to be a greater occultist than all of them (certainly I am unlikely to be as prolific a

---

[92] See, for instance, my essay on free inquiry elsewhere in this volume, titled "Odian Wandering Among the 'Ettins.'"

[93] I have found many other Grails in my questing. In this volume, see my essay, "Moldavite as the Stone and the Grail." Outside of it, see my essay, Westcoat, "Runes for the Grails" and also my academically published article, Westcoat, "The Valknut: Heart of the Slain?"

[94] For a chapter-length discussion of many of the castle's occultist visitors, see Siepe, "Esoteric Perspectives," 207–49.

writer as the greatest of them), but my travels on the Road to Monsalvat are not yet over.

What else then? A long time has passed, perhaps enough time that the World of Tradition which inspired the symbol now seeks to redeem it and see it put to new use in the days and years ahead. Perhaps it is King Arthur himself who is almost healed and ready to return with his Knights of the Round Table. The Realm of Spirit operates on a timetable of which we know not. But the astrologically minded may note that the symbol had its birth quite closely aligning with the last entrance of Uranus into the sign of Gemini in August 1941, for the North Tower was under construction at that time. Now, roughly 84 years later, Uranus again entered Gemini in July 2025, in time for the rebirth of this symbol to the world. Perhaps the old colonel would approve of such astrological timing.

What shall it be used for now? Those who only dwell in the mundane world should be very wary, in light of the rampant misuse that those of no spiritual inclination have made of the symbol. Invoking the Round Table with this symbol will not save today's villains any more than it saved the SS. People should be especially cautious of wearing it. What was indicated earlier in *Wigalois* regarding Gawain's son having it on his shield ("Whoever succeeded in this wore the Round Table so that one could know that he had a seat there") is also stated explicitly and a bit differently in Robert de Boron's cycle. There, we have additional textual authority for seeing the insignia of the Round Table as something that is borne by a great many knights, far more than just the 12 knights (or however many) that are best or closest enough to actually sit at it with Arthur:

> [Arthur] said: ". . . The twelve peers of my court will sit in the twelve seats; but I want you to know that all who attend my feast and wish to stay with me will be forever of the company of the Round Table, and as a mark of high honour wherever they may go, each will carry the Round Table's pennon or device.'"
>
> This announcement caused a great stir, and all the barons of the court were overjoyed, for they longed to be known as members of the Round Table. . . .

> . . . And so many knights and damsels were there that the king presented five thousand four hundred robes and devices of the Round Table.[95]

That's a fairly sizable company! And it suggests that many could indeed hope to join the Round Table, perhaps even today. But in what ways may one today become worthy enough to claim to be among their number and wear the icon of the Round Table in the present age? What voices from Spirit speak with Arthur's authority to summon new Knights to the Round Table? That is a discussion that I won't enter into here.

But esotericist individuals and groups have already been working with the symbol in non-fascist capacities, though surely with only nebulous ideas of what it really was. Perhaps some of these people suspected that the Round Table was at the root of the symbol, but did not realize the extent to which an actual case could be made for it. This essay will give them something new to consider.[96] The best esoteric schools encourage their members to quest for spiritual development and the higher self. The metaphor of Knighthood and Grail questing is a valuable one for self-transformation that they and others make use of, and having such a powerful symbol of the Round Table and Grail may be a great boon to the Great Work—for those who are worthy.

Final Remarks

Some will accept nothing less than actual source documentation from the SS as an explanation for the Wewelsburg symbol. But I'm confident mine is the answer, and I am saying that if such documentation were ever found, it would bear out my explanation

---

[95] Robert de Boron, *Merlin and the Grail*, 116–17.

[96] To mention just one possibility: the Round Table Sun Wheel is positioned directly above the "Roots of the World Tree" swastika in Wewelsburg's Gruft. One might thus experiment with the notion of roots feeding and nourishing the Round Table. But note that Wolfram's *Parzival* has the Grail receiving food from Spirit above in the form of a dove that brings a small white wafer down to it every Good Friday, which would be an appropriate opposition to incorporate in a Polarian synthesis of the two.

in *all* its particulars. And if such documentation is never found, then mine may well be the best explanation there will ever be. For those who don't like this one, I challenge them to come up with alternative explanations, although as far as the Arthurian hypothesis is concerned, what I've done here probably can't be beaten.

Some will be horrified at what I've done here, because "Evil Nazis!" or because "My Aryan Black Sun!" Some undoubtedly will wish this symbol remained an unsolved mystery through the end of time. They profane the Solar Ideal of the Round Table. All of them need to get over themselves.

Some will come across this essay and still wonder what all the fuss was about. That's okay! That's far from the worst view to take of all this. The light of the Grail may yet come to them when they are ready.

Some will come across this essay and be delighted to see a great mystery solved and a strange new world opened up thereby. And a few will look at the Round Table Sun Wheel with fresh eyes, see that a new road has opened to Monsalvat, and take up the Sword of Tradition. They will join the Great Quest of those who know that the Light of Spirit still shines upon our darkened World, sometimes from the most unexpected places, though most cannot see it. It is the Quest for the Grail.

Acknowledgments

Many thanks go to Stephen Flowers, David Lovewell, Michael Moynihan, Herne Siegmann, and others unnamed who reviewed drafts of this essay. Special thanks go to Herne Siegmann for some research materials. Finally, thanks also go to the Internet Archive, where I found several books that would have been difficult to get.

Works Cited

Ackermann, Josef. *Heinrich Himmler als Ideologe*. Göttingen: Musterschmidt-Verlag, 1970.

Beyond Room 313. "Wewelsburg Without the Nonsense - Along with the Secret of the Black Sun." Video, 2019. <www.youtube.com/watch?v=_JvH54k5u_M>.

"Black Sun." *Wikimedia Commons.* Image by Blacksonne, with changes of color and addition of a core by Eirik Westcoat. <commons.wikimedia.org/wiki/File:The_Black_Sun.svg>. License: <creativecommons.org/licenses/by-sa/4.0/>.

BnF Manuscrits Français 112, folio 5r. "A Vision of the Grail" by Évrard d'Espinques. *Gallica Digital Library.* <gallica.bnf.fr/ark:/12148/btv1b8527589h/f13.item>.

BnF Manuscrits Français 116, folio 610v. "A Vision of the Grail" by Évrard d'Espinques. *Gallica Digital Library.* <gallica.bnf.fr/ark:/12148/btv1b6000093b/f78.item>.

BnF Manuscrits Français 120 at Bibliothèque nationale de France. Available at <archivesetmanuscrits.bnf.fr/ark:/12148/cc42954c/ca59913945024303>.

BnF Manuscrits Français 120, folio 524v. "The Vision of the Grail" by Maître des Clères Femmes. *Gallica Digital Library.* <gallica.bnf.fr/ark:/12148/btv1b84920806/f114>.

Brown, James H. *Imagining the Text: Ekphrasis and Envisioning Courtly Identity in Wirnt von Gravenberg's Wigalois.* Leiden: Brill, 2016.

Comfort, W. W., trans. *The Quest of the Holy Grail.* Old French Series. Cambridge, Ontario: In Parentheses, 2000. <www.yorku.ca/inpar/quest_comfort.pdf>. (Original publication: Toronto: J.M. Dent & Sons, 1926.)

Flowers, Stephen E., and Michael Moynihan. *The Secret King: The Myth and Reality of Nazi Occultism.* 2nd edition. Los Angeles: Feral House / Dominion, 2007.

Goodrick-Clarke, Nicholas. *Black Sun: Aryan Cults, Esoteric Nazism and the Politics of Identity.* New York and London: New York University Press, 2002.

Goodrick-Clarke, Nicholas. *The Occult Roots of Nazism: Secret Aryan Cults and Their Influence on Nazi Ideology.* London: Tauris Parke Paperbacks, 2004. [Originally published 1985.]

Hunger, Ulrich. *Die Runenkunde im Dritten Reich.* Frankfurt: Peter Lang, 1984.

Hüser, Karl. *Wewelsburg 1933 bis 1945: Kult- und Torrorstätte der SS—Eine Dokumentation.* Paderborn: Verlag Boniftius-Druckerei, 1982.

hwo/Alamy. Photos of the Wewelsburg Sun Wheel and Gruft. Image IDs FW65CW and FW65CH respectively, licensed from <www.alamy.com>.

"King Arthur's Round Table at Winchester Castle, Winchester, Hampshire, England." *Wikimedia Commons*. Photo by Rsnourse. <commons.wikimedia.org/wiki/File:King_Arthur's_Round_Table_at_Winchester_Castle,_Winchester,_Hampshire,_England.png>. License: <creativecommons.org/licenses/by-sa/4.0/>.

"*Kingdoms of Camelot*." Wikipedia. Accessed May 13, 2025. <en.wikipedia.org/wiki/Kingdoms_of_Camelot>.

John-Stucke, Kirsten. "22. September 1934 - Übernahme der Wewelsburg durch Heinrich Himmler." *Internet-Portal „Westfälische Geschichte."* <lwl.org/westfaelische-geschichte/portal/Internet/input_felder/langDatensatz_ebene4.php?urlID=497&url_tabelle=tab_websegmente>.

John-Stucke, Kirsten. "Himmler's Plans and Activities in Wewelsburg." In *Myths of Wewelsburg Castle: Facts and Fiction*, edited by Kirsten John-Stucke and Daniela Siepe, 1–32.

John-Stucke, Kirsten, and Daniela Siepe, eds. *Myths of Wewelsburg Castle: Facts and Fiction*. Translated by David Antal and James Bell. Publications of the Kreismuseum Wewelsburg, Vol. 12. Paderborn: Brill Schöningh, 2022.

Longerich, Peter. *Heinrich Himmler*. Translated by Jeremy Noakes and Lesley Sharpe. Oxford: Oxford University Press, 2012.

Loomis, Roger Sherman, with Laura Hibbard Loomis. *Arthurian Legends in Medieval Art*. London: Oxford University Press; and New York: MLA of America, 1938. <archive.org/details/arthurianlegends00loom/>.

LTK 537 at Leiden University Libraries. Available at <hdl.handle.net/1887.1/item:1615443>.

LTK 537, folio 36v. "Some Wheel of Fortune Depictions." *Leiden University Libraries Digital Collections*. <hdl.handle.net/1887.1/item:1615638>.

LTK 537, opening 4. "Wigalois Round Table." *Leiden University Libraries Digital Collections*. <hdl.handle.net/1887.1/item:1615587>.

McCloud, Russell. [Pseudonym of Stephan Mögle-Stadel et al.] *Die Schwarze Sonne von Tashi Lhunpo*. 4th ed. Engerda, Germany: Arun-Verlag, 1999. [Originally published 1991.]

"Obergruppenführersaal mit Schwarzer Sonne, Wewelsburg." *Wikimedia Commons*. Photo by Dirk Vorderstraße. <commons.wikimedia.org/wiki/File:Obergruppenführersaal_mit_Schwarzer_Sonne,_Wewelsburg_(10573256656).jpg>. License: <creativecommons.org/licenses/by/2.0/>.

"Parsifal 1882 Act 3." *Wikimedia Commons*. <commons.wikimedia.org/wiki/File:Parsifal_1882_Act3_Joukowsky_NGO4p119.jpg>.

Pontolillo, James. *The Black Sun Unveiled: Genesis and Development of a Modern National Socialist Mythos*. Kingsport, MA: Morryster and Sons Publishing, 2013.

Pontolillo, James. *The Black Sun Revisited: Further Chapters in the Development of a Modern National Socialist Mythos*. Kingsport, MA: Morryster and Sons Publishing, 2017.

Renner, Dorothee. *Die durchbrochenen Zierscheiben der Merowingerzeit*. Mainz: Verlag des Römisch-Germanischen Zentralmuseums, 1970.

"Resin Statuary Examples." For instance, <kingdomofarms.com/products/knights-of-the-round-table-statue> and <fairyglen.com/products/king-arthur-the-knights-of-the-round-table>.

Robert de Boron. *Merlin and the Grail: Joseph of Arimathea, Merlin, Perceval: The Trilogy of Prose Romances Attributed to Robert de Boron*. Translated by Nigel Bryant. Cambridge: D. S. Brewer, 2001.

Siepe, Daniela. "Esoteric Perspectives on Wewelsburg Castle: Reception in 'Satanist Circles." In *Myths of Wewelsburg Castle: Facts and Fiction*, edited by Kirsten John-Stucke and Daniela Siepe, 207–49.

Siepe, Daniela. "The 'Grail Castle' of the SS? The Creation of Legends about Wewelsburg Castle in Scholarly and Popular-Science Literature." In *Myths of Wewelsburg Castle: Facts and Fiction*, edited by Kirsten John-Stucke and Daniela Siepe, 33–93.

Siepe, Daniela. "The Sun Wheel as a 'Black Sun' in Wewelsburg Castle's *Obergruppenführer* Hall." In *Myths of Wewelsburg Castle: Facts and Fiction*, edited by Kirsten John-Stucke and Daniela Siepe, 143–62.

Sünner, Rüdiger. *Schwarze Sonne: Entfesselung und Mißbrauch der Mythen in Nationalsozialismus und rechter Esoterik*. Freiburg: Herder / Spektrum, 1999.

"Swords United." *Know Your Meme*. Accessed May 13, 2025. <knowyourmeme.com/memes/swords-united>.

"Swords United." *Meming Wiki*. Accessed May 13, 2025. <en.meming.world/wiki/Swords_United>.

Thomas, Neil. *Wirnt von Gravenberg's Wigalois: Intertextuality and Interpretation*. Cambridge: D. S. Brewer, 2005.

Westcoat, Eirik. "Runes for the Grails: Creating Old English Rune Poem Stanzas for Cweorð, Calc, Stān, and Gār." In *Eagle's Mead*, 249–89, 178–82 (poem translation). Long Branch, PA: Skaldic Eagle Press, 2019.

Westcoat, Eirik. *The Skaldic Eagle*. <theskaldiceagle.com>.

Westcoat, Eirik. "The Valknut: Heart of the Slain?" *Odroerir: The Heathen Journal* 3.2 (November 2015): 1–23.

Wiligut, Karl Maria [Jarl Widar]. "Gotos Raunen—Runenwissen!" *Hagal* 11, no. 7 (1934): 7–15. (English translation in Flowers and Moynihan, *The Secret King*, 85–98.)

Wiligut, Karl Maria [Jarl Widar]. "Tyrkreiszeichen und Sternbilder." *Hagal* 12, no. 4 (1935): 56–58. (English translation in Flowers and Moynihan, *The Secret King*, 112–14.)

Wirnt von Gravenberch. *Wigalois: Der Ritter mit dem Rade*. Edited by George Friederich Benecke. Berlin: G. Reimer, 1819. <archive.org/details/wigaloisderritte00wirnuoft/>.

Wirnt von Graftenberg. *Wigalois: The Knight of Fortune's Wheel*. Translated by J. W. Thomas. Lincoln, NE: University of Nebraska Press, 1997. <archive.org/details/wigaloisknightof0000wirn>.

Wolfram von Eschenbach. *Parzival and Titurel*. Translated by Cyril Edwards. Oxford: Oxford University Press, 2006.